MY STORIES

Damir Ibrišimović

Order this book online at www.trafford.com
or email orders@trafford.com

Most Trafford titles are also available at major online book retailers.

Note for Librarians: A cataloguing record for this book is available from Library
and Archives Canada at www.collectionscanada.ca/amicus/index-e.html

Printed in Victoria, BC, Canada.

ISBN: 978-1-4251-8839-9 (sc)

*Our mission is to efficiently provide the world's finest, most comprehensive book publishing
service, enabling every author to experience success. To find out how to publish your book, your
way, and have it available worldwide, visit us online at www.trafford.com*

Trafford rev. 8/14/2009

 www.trafford.com

North America & international
toll-free: 1 888 232 4444 (USA & Canada)
phone: 250 383 6864 ♦ fax: 812 355 4082

Contents

To Fleur

THE BOOKLET YOU HOLD IS rather a workbook. There is room for you to comment and weave your own stories. My Stories are without the ballast of guards against possible critiques. Ballast of references is also minimised and every effort was made to avoid jargon.

The most of the stories are related to each other on many levels outlining a structure that would be hard to express without poetic-like language. The word story, for example, is often a metaphor for meanings quite different from stories we share with each other. The word story is also a metaphor for our habitual thought, feeling or action that determine in many ways how we see the world around us. On the level of our cells (or single cell organism), word story should be understood as genome or epigenome. And there are other meanings…

There are also other poetic-like tools. Repeated reading with so induced variety of meanings will establish the intended coherent structure. And I hope that you will enjoy discovering it…

I also hope for your active participation. If my story on workable ethics rings true, you are morally obliged to respond. And if you agree with my story on aesthetics, your stories will artfully tell more with less.

Your responses will be welcomed at my discussion group:

http://tech.groups.yahoo.com/group/Imagine_Knowledge/

With enough substantive responses, I will be able to plan the second edition that will incorporate them – with authors' approvals. This really can be the greatest peer review ever attempted…

It is likely that my stories will challenge some of yours. And this might be a difficult challenge. Take the challenge. The result could be stories better than mine.

Oh, one more thing. As Croatian who learned English late, some expressions might turn out clumsy. Hopefully, the intended meaning is not affected…

We live in an infinite universe full of unique phenomena. And each phenomenon is infinitely different from all others. Every human is unique. Every apple is unique. Emerging from the previous, every moment of our lives is unique. And time builds upon itself...

To prove to ourselves the existence of this impossible infinite universe, all we need is to open and close our eyes. It is quite simple — open your eyes and try to remember as much as you can of what you see right now. Now, close your eyes and try to imagine the same. Did you notice the difference? No matter how vivid an imagination and photographic memory you might have, the difference is enormous and impossible to express. The open eyes world is full of infinitely rich sensations that are not present in the closed eyes world. To deal with this infinite, open eyes world, we need our stories about it in our closed eyes world.

Since our species emerged we have weaved our stories and shared them with others. Every moment of our lives leaves emotionally charged memories in us. A stronger emotional charge will carry our memories for a while enabling us to weave a new story of ours. And our stories live much longer than any emotional charge. Told or untold, our stories weave the cloth we are made of. And this cloth enables us to remember, to see, to think and to act. As we tell our stories to others, we also weave the invisible fabric our cultures are made of. And well-woven stories of ours may live a long, a very long, life in our culture. This knowledge of how we weave our stories – the Know Thyself Discipline – will also enable us to weave our stories better.

PSYCHOLOGISTS AND NEUROLOGISTS (RATHER THAN neuroscientists; tautology) were dumbfounded with first glimpses of the two universes we live in. They found no differences in our brain activity as we see or imagine the same. They could not find in our brains even a trace of the rich sensations we experience with our eyes open.[1] Follow-ups only confirmed that our brain is not much more than a storyteller, sometimes artful and sometimes dull. And this storyteller lights up when listening to an artful story told or written, almost as we are actually there and see what the story tells. Thus, our brain is dethroned as the centre of everything we experience. But, our brain is crowned again – with a lesser crown though.

But where are we – the whole of us? Well, this could be answered only with: "The whole is more than a sum of its parts." And our brain is only one part of us. The whole of us brings us to an intriguing theory – Complex Adaptive Systems Theory or simply – complexity.[2] The main idea is that a system gains a property through the interplay of its parts – a property that cannot be derived from properties of its parts. It is like saltines that cannot be derived from properties of sodium or chloride. This is the meaning of "more" in "the whole is more than the sum of its parts".

The whole of us includes our eyes, ears, nose, taste buds and all other parts of our body together with our brain. And when we sleep, our most vivid dreams are marked by the very high activity of our eyes[3] – indicating the contribution of our eyes to the vividness of our dreams.

---

1   Nancy Kanwisher and Kathleen O'Craven scanned brain activity of subjects who were imagining or actually seeing images.
2   Although not going far enough, Klaus Mainzer's "Thinking in Complexity" is still the best introduction into complexity.
3   Rapid eye movement or REM phase.

SPLIT-BRAIN PATIENTS OFFER A WEALTH of data for how we see.[4] The halves of the brains of split-brain patients do not talk to each other. And if the left eye does not see the same the right eye does, what is seen is recognised by each of the halves separately. Knowing this, psychologists devised a clever experiment. For example, they presented a picture of a shovel to the left eye only. At the same time they presented a picture of a chicken to the right eye. The subject was then presented with toys that included a shovel and a chicken to choose what they have seen. They chose correctly, but the reasoning they offered for the choice was perplexing. All the answers were in style – "you need a shovel to clean up a chicken shed"…

Most of us do not have our brains split. Our halves talk to each other and we do not have many shovels and chickens – do we? Hmm… We (pedestrians) stop at a red light even if there are no cars to be seen on both sides. What kind of answers will we give if asked why we do not cross the road? The first will be that the light is red. If pressed with the fact that there are no cars, we would probably say that we did not look. And if pressed about why we did not look, we would probably say that we were thinking about something else. We probably would not say that we stopped first and then started to think about something else…

Our "red light behaviour" is only a tiny example of a symptom we all demonstrate. And we demonstrate everything, with all contradictions, that is happening in our closed eyes world in every manner we can: faster heart beat, odour, sweat, involuntary micro twitches of facial muscles, body posture etc. etc. In theory, we could build equipment that would measure all these demonstrations of our stories – and pinpoint the conflicting ones.

Unfortunately, we do not have such equipment to help us pinpoint answers in the style – you need a shovel to clean up a chicken shed… We will probably not have anything like this imagined equipment in the foreseeable future – and even if we have it, how to interpret the mountains of data will be a problem. The only feasible path to detection of shovels and chickens in our stories is introspection and reconciliation between stories.[5]

---

4   Surgical intervention that disables communication between halves of the brain is sometimes necessary to reduce seizures some epileptics experience.

5   I did my best to eliminate shovels and chickens from My Stories. But I'm sure that I missed many. If you find some – please – do not hesitate to let me know.

To clean up the chicken shed we need to tease our stories out with intent. Shovels and chickens are already ridiculous enough and habit breaking exercises[6] will start on their own...

But, our individual stories full of shovels and chickens are just a minor issue when compared with the volumes of stories full of shovels and chickens generated by our culture nowadays...

This is also true for our scientific disciplines divided by iron curtains. We have no choice but to roll up our sleeves, take the shovel and clean up the chicken shed...

---

6   See story on Creativity.

PEOPLE WERE CLOSELY OBSERVING EVERYTHING even before Homo sapiens started to migrate. But during migrations they learned to observe more methodically and efficiently. And since then our observational skills evolved with us and our culture.

The last evolutionary leap of our observational skills peaked in the Age of Reason – the 17th & 18th centuries. And since then we have been perfecting something called the scientific method. However, when we ask scientists to tell us what the scientific method is, we get as many lengthy answers as there are scientists. And answers could be so simple…

In the open eyes world, scientists translate their sensations into observations – data. Reflecting on their observations, they form an opinion (explanation), technically called theory. This opinion suppose to predict what they will observe in the future. But, since nothing can be entirely predicted, future observations always yield nagging anomalies. And our scientists are annoyed until somebody offers hope with a different opinion, technically called a hypothesis. And they again sink themselves into the open eyes world to observe. And if the new opinion removes some of those nuisances, the potential theory will be born.

However, methodical observations need a parallel mechanism to become the scientific method. This mechanism is called peer review. When one or more scientists observe on the basis of the new opinion and their observations confirm this new opinion (hypothesis), other scientists sift through their data to confirm or reject the new opinion. But confirmation does not mean that it is over. Other scientists start their own observations to confirm or reject the potential theory. Only if the new opinion passes all these verifications, will the scientists dare to commit regicide.

The theory is dead; long live the theory!

If you ask a scientist, the scientific method is the only way we can objectively speak about our open eyes universe. And, to a degree, they are right. But there are hidden dangers in this "objectivity", even scientists admit.

The first danger is in peer reviews of scientists who believe in the same new opinion. And all is fine if there are scientists who favour another new opinion. Debates flare up until dust settles with one down or with a third opinion left standing. Furthermore, if the same thinkers represent majority, they are often tempted to ignore a competing opinion (and there are always some). Majority slumbers producing much of the same and voices of few have very hard time to wake the majority up.

The second danger is in iron curtains between sciences. These iron curtains are woven from theories that are entirely incomprehensible in other scientific disciplines. Biologists of today would be hopeless as peer reviewers for and as testers of an opinion (theory) of quantum physicists. This narrows the selection of peer reviewers to the same thinkers within a single discipline only. And our disciplines further break up into sub-disciplines – threatening to become separate sciences.

The third danger is in "objectivity" itself. In the Age of Reason we firmly believed that everything we saw in our open eyes universe is exactly as we saw it. Nobody thought that our data (observations) could be biased. Nobody thought that we see what we expect[7] to see – based upon previous experiences. And our data became "objective". But this danger will be exposed gradually as we go through stories of how we see and why we see the way we do.

---

7   See Intent and related stories.

BEFORE I START TO WEAVE my little (scientific) stories I have to define the Know Thyself Discipline – what it is, what it does and how it does what it does. I'll also outline obstacles to this kind of science. So, let's start with the first one.

For far too long, scientists looked at human beings (and other beings) from the outside[8]. This was only partly justifiable, for how we behave does tell a lot about us.[9] However, scientists' cooperation with the views of subjects from within became necessary – but not scientists' views from within. (Sic)

The Know Thyself Discipline is introspective verification of scientific findings about us (from the outside). It only completes the cooperative cycle scientists initiated. The only difference is that we are not mere (unqualified) subjects only. With keen introspective verifications we can become their peers in the peer review process.

The second obstacle is in the refusal of scientists to accept the existence of the open eyes universe. But this requires an unheard of type of evidence – subjective evidence. As long we are not accepted as their peers, this type of evidence will be "unacceptable"[10]. And peer review could be so simple – all scientists need to do is to sit down, open and then close their eyes and confirm this "finding"…

The Know Thyself Discipline embraces our open, wide-open eyes universe. This is where all of us, scientists and non-scientists, test our hypotheses. And many non-scientists can be very thorough in their tests and observations…

Introspective experiments and observations are necessary to map our views from within with views from without.

However, we need to be qualified – and to be qualified does not necessarily mean to own a paper called a diploma[11]. To qualify we need to put together a comprehensive

---

8   See The 18th Century – The Duck.
9   In theory, we manifest everything that is happening in our closed eyes world. However, in practice, the equipment that will measure every minute manifestation of ours is impossible to even imagine. And who would be able to interpret mountains of so obtained data? From outside we can have clues only – to lead us in our investigations from within. Willy-nilly scientists are already practicing know thyself science when interpreting observations about us from outside…
10   I do hope that scientists will realise how ridiculous this situation is. Humph, they might get ideas, though, to hide themselves, so that we do not learn that they are doing their observations in the open eyes universe.
11   Diplomas are often just a certificate saying that you can write, talk and think in a language (jargon) of a science that is often incomprehensible in another. Minimising jargon would result in much better qualified scientists – even scientists without diplomas. Wouldn't be wonderful to have artists, philosophers and others discussing science with scientists on an equal footing – again?

picture about us in simple words everybody can understand. And we need to root this picture solidly in scientific findings from without and our experiences from within.

As scientists do, I will weave my opinions (hypotheses) here into a comprehensive picture of us. And I offer them to all of you, scientists and non-scientists, to test them and map them with your own observations.

FOR A LONG TIME OUR stories about "how we see" and "why we see the way we do" were based on Descartes' story – there is a little us, sitting somewhere in our brain, that is in charge. The "little us in charge" is the one that receives all our sensations and thinks, feels and commands our body to carry out a reaction or an action – the little us who does all of the seeing, thinking, feeling and acting for us…

Neurologists (rather than neuroscientists; tautology) also started to look for this "little us in charge" in our brain. With psychologists and a variety of scanning machines they also looked at how our brains "lights up" when we look at or imagine the same, speak, or meditate etc. After many discoveries in their pockets, scientists are now very reluctant to venture into the philosophers' la-la land of consciousness. They could not find this "little us" (consciousness?) in the brain.

Each new find threw the "little us in charge" and the philosophers' consciousness out of balance. The capacity of our consciousness was measured first. It turned out that we can be conscious of up to seven symbols at one time.[12] Then Dr. Benjamin Libet made the only possible assumption – we are conscious of what we are conscious of – and nothing else. He knew that each physical action requires at least 0.8 seconds of brain activity before the action is carried out.[13] And he decided to do some time measurements on patients during surgery on their brains – when our consciousness decides to carry out an action?

The results of the series of various measurements astonished scientists and philosophers. Apparently our consciousness does not initiate any of our physical actions. All measurements indicated that our consciousness can only step-in half a second **after** our brain was active in preparation to execute the action. And it can only step-in to prevent or veto the action.[14] But who or what then initiates an action of ours? Can we then consciously decide on anything? Do we have a free will – at all?

In this total confusion, Nancy Kanwisher excitedly reported how brain scans reveal what a subject is actually seeing or imagining. With very high levels of accuracy she and her team could tell if a person was seeing or imagining a face or a scene. Unfortunately, in her report, she failed to notice how significant the absence of differ-

---

12   The figure varies depending on the type of measurement, but the most generous figure was 40 – a
       far cry from the richness of the open eyes world.
13   Technical term – readiness potential.
14   Dr Libet did not take into account that his experiments were restricted to voluntary physical actions
       only. Missing this dimension, his interpretation of measurements did not take this "voluntary" into
       account – but this is a separate story of mine. (See Intent story.)

ences between imagined and actually seen is. Brain scans of imagined (closed eyes) and actually seen (open eyes) were virtually identical. In other words, **the infinitely rich sensations of our open eyes world were nowhere to be seen in our brain.** Obviously intrigued with this observation of mine (published on my website), she performed another experiment[15]. I guess that she was surprised with the results – it turned out that we see category first and then fill it in with details.

Descartes' "little us in charge" is our old, 17th Century story that cannot survive all these findings. Many other stories of ours built upon the "little us in charge" cannot survive unscathed either. So, let's the "little us in charge" domino fall on others…

---

15   Findings were published by Psychological Science (Vol 16, No.2).

WHEN WE OPEN OUR EYES we are embraced by our universe that fills us with rich sensations – sensations talking about infinity of unique phenomena. Nothing ever happens or appears exactly the same as before in this universe. Even physicists agree that the existence of two entirely identical wavicles (**wav**e/par**ticle**) would be against the laws of physics. (While saying so, they will turn to their computer models of a closed universe full of repeatable phenomena …)

There are many who still believe in the 17th Century story. Although incapable of replicating anything entirely, they maintain the story about a cause and effect driven universe. They maintain this story in the belief that there are hidden causes we do not know of. Unable to replicate, they had to accept a little devil that spoils an otherwise perfectly predictable outcome – chance. Yet, a deep belief that the universe is like a divine clock devised and put into motion by God or erupting into existence in the Big Bang[16], remains. There must be a beginning at the beginning, mustn't there?

Old beliefs (stories) can only be countered with new beliefs (stories) that better reflect the infinities we are surrounded with. After all, we are talking here about our open eyes universe – an infinite universe full of unique phenomena.

We cannot say much more about our open eyes universe. Unique is, well, unique – and infinite does not have limits. All we can do is live in it and articulate our stories about it; enjoy the prior and think about the latter.

Fortunately, we can tell much more about how this infinite universe, full of unique phenomena, is reflected in our brain. We can tell our stories about it. And we can artfully tell more with less.

---

16 The latest fashion is re-cycling, Big Bounce universe. Math looks nice, but the theory will be hard, likely impossible to verify. Like multiverse, we might have here just an attempt to justify previous mathematical models in a different form.

WE NEED TO RE-COGNISE EVERYTHING in our environment as quickly as possible. And our brain, cooperating with our eyes and ears, does a marvellous job. And although brain scanning is restricted to labs, we do have enough for a comprehensive story about how our brain lights up as we wander and wonder[17] in our open eyes world.

Every moment of our lives, we non-consciously expect to see this or that when we turn around a corner. And, if we do not expect a danger, we will turn confidently and see what we expected to see. And these expectations are based upon what we already saw before when we turned around the same corner.[18] With a good mind map we can safely go around and see what we expect (intent) to see. And very few things need the attention of our consciousness. Even if we are heading to a bakery, recognition of it does not need the attention of our consciousness.

When we are on familiar ground, groups of our brain cells dance detailed dances even before we turn the corner. There is a detailed dance for the bakery; a detailed dance for exactly there; a detailed dance for if it is open, etc. And when we turn the corner we recognise most of the things in an instant. And, in most cases, more vague expectations for people, cars, cats, dogs etc. will gain specifics quickly.[19]

As long everything goes as expected, our consciousness needs to attend only recognitions of vague expectations that gained importance through specifics. We recognise a friend, for example. Specifics of a beautiful woman we do not know will be drawn to our eyes even before her beauty filters into our consciousness.

The unexpected can be dangerous and this will draw the attention of our consciousness. But the unexpected belongs rather to cognition than to re-cognition. Recognition is rather based on precise stories (habits) of our mind map.

---

17   Did you pause for a moment when you read "wander and wonder"? If you did, you paused because you paid more attention to the pronunciation than to the print. And repeated, silent utterance did not sound right.

18   See Intent story.

19   Sometimes even specifics are unimportant. There was an experiment in which a stranger would ask for directions. In the middle of the reply they were rudely disrupted by two people carrying a door between them. Many of the subjects did not notice that another person replaced the stranger while they were "disrupted". They simply continued…

Important

This story is about how we re-cognise — i.e. how we make sense and orient ourselves to a familiar territory. It is not about seeing infinities of our open eyes universe. It is about how these infinities are reflected in our closed eyes universe that helps us to navigate through our open eyes world.

WE DO NOT HAVE MIND maps for unfamiliar territories. Our expectations are vague, sometimes very vague – like in labs during experiments trying to discern how we see. Cognition is learning[20] how to re-cognise (see). Our cognition story has to look into the amazing job our brain, eyes and ears do, very quickly, in cooperation.

The secret of the speed of our cognition is in rapid dialogues between our brain, eyes and ears. And the dialogue between our brain and our eyes probably starts with vague expectations that could be translated like this: Eyes of ours is it an object? Is it dark? Is it opaque? Is it far? ... To ask all these simultaneous questions, groups of our brain cells dance their inquisitive dances. Depending on the answers our eyes and ears provide, more specific inquisitive dances start – quickly building up details about what the object is.

With enough details our brain can tell us: "This is the tail of a fox hidden under that reddish bush. And the fox appears to be pretending to be dead[21]." The brain tells us all this by interpreting different dances of different groups of brain cells for each of the detail told.[22] And all of these dances happen simultaneously before we are able to put them into words. And when we are putting these dances into words, we leave out many details our brain cells told us through their dances.

On the entirely unfamiliar ground our eyes dart from one thing we consider important to another. At the same time our ears are trying to map sounds with what we see. And each time our eyes stop at something, cognitive dialogues start. And each time details building moments will pass.

Although we are able to cognise the most on the unfamiliar ground, we need time to form a reliable mind map. We need to visit and dream about the same place to create a new story (habit) about it.

However, a warning is necessary. Even on very familiar ground, precise expectations about what and where to see can fail. When very precise expectations fail, we will actually fail to see. If we expect that our eraser bounced off precisely there under

---

20 See Weaving New Stories. Note also that cognition is a kind of re-cognition, but re-cognition of details that build the picture as a whole.

21 This is how the fox earned its fame.

22 Fox cells dance fox dance for whole fox; tail cells dance tail dance for the whole of tail; etc. Some painters (Paul Cézanne, for example) tried to express this wholistic aspect of our visual perception. Wholism of our auditory perception could be seen in syncopation, for example. (Wholistic and wholism are coined words.)

the desk, we will fail to see the eraser even if it is only centimetres away.[23] Only when we make failed expectations vague enough will we be able to see where the eraser actually bounced off.

---

23   Our erasers have a funny habit of bouncing off in unexpected ways often fooling our expectations about their final resting place.

Although (fortunately) rare, there are moments in our lives in which we do not have time to think about what we see. These are the moments when our or someone else's life is in danger. These are the moments when we are pure action – the action driven by intuition and reflexes alone – the action when our consciousness is a powerless observer without any chance to intend or veto.

Such events are filled to the brim with emotions. Only later, when the danger is fended off, can we reflect on these moments and notice what we did not notice before. And we will dream about these moments – and literally practice our reflexive actions to be better prepared in the future for such moments.[24]

Unfortunately, our lives in luxury and safety often do not demand practicing our reflexes and intuition. Only certain professions, like in the army for example, impose practicing our reflexes[25] – drills. And without good reflexes and intuition we are likely to freeze and die in such a moment that might be waiting for us right now around that corner…

---

24   Doctors in emergency wards and other emergency professionals have gone through such moments so many times that their intuition and reflexes became a routine – habit. And they continue to perfect their intuition and reflexes on a daily basis – even in their dreams.

25   Unfortunately, drills in the army do not require developing intuition and we have often too much "collateral damage". The police do a much better job with drills that distinguish between "good" and "bad" guys.

Each cell of our body needs intent – intent to tune itself with all other cells of our body. But each of our cells also needs a metronome – an internal clock to keep itself in sync with others. We have found evidence of these internal clocks. We have also found a master circadian clock in our brains – a conductor who oversees all this tick-tacking. But, for now, we do not have evidence for the most important part – intent.

All of our actions depend on our cells dancing in sync to the rhythms of our stories. And whenever we learn a new dance for example, we create a new story with a rhythm for our cells to guide them in their dances. Our stories are like music to the ears of our cells. All we need is to recall them (intent) and they will dance their learned – habitual – dances.

As our cells dance we also dance with each other in our daily moments. And depending on how well we have learned the stories of our culture, we dance almost flawlessly. We gather for a meeting at about the same time. We tune to each other at work, at home, in the theatre, etc. And we (our culture) dance – sometimes clumsily, stepping on each other's toes and sometimes artfully winning the day…

Artful dance in our culture (team) demands that we tune ourselves to each other to very high levels of perfection. If we do this, we can artfully dance together, like a basketball team when a player passes the ball to his teammate without even looking. And behind all this the interplay of our stories will enable the emergence of the stories of our culture – music to our ears — just as our individual stories are music to the ears of our cells.

We are quite good at tuning ourselves to the rhythm of other humans around us.[26] We do our business by tuning to the needs of others. And we expect others to tune to our needs. We tune ourselves to the needs of our families. And we teach our kids to tune themselves to our needs and the needs of others. Whenever this tuning does not happen, it hurts.

---

26 Unfortunately, we forgot to tune ourselves with the rest of our environment and the resulting noise is far from anything like music.

OUR OPEN EYES UNIVERSE EMBRACES us and fills us with infinitely rich sensations. And we re-act in this universe of ours with the whole of our body — with every single cell of our body.

This re-action we call emotion that is almost entirely metabolic in its nature. The greater the change in our metabolism, the more vivid the memories we will have. Our stories are under the command of our storyteller, but they will also reflect metabolic changes we went through at that moment. And this helps us to almost relive a moment of our past when a scent, for example, hits our nose. What we were conscious of then we become conscious of again – and reflect[27]…

Large metabolic changes can, in the future, induce a reflection on a moment of our past longer than a half a second. And this enables our consciousness to reflect on the moment of our past for a few moments of our now. With this we might become conscious of things we were not conscious of then.

Sensations reflected in metabolic changes will carry their reflections to every single cell of ours. And these reflections will be further reflected in our genome and epigenome[28], to carry together with our culture our personal experiences (stories) to our posterity.

Emotions and rhythm that carry them are best observed in a small universe that emulates our open eyes universe – live theatre. Actors play their bodies like fine instruments, constantly tuning with each other and with the audience. And masters can synchronise themselves so much that the whole of the theatre resonates with emotions in the same rhythm.

*   *   *

Artfully told stories by stage acting masters are full of emotional charges.[29] This ensures that every single person in the audience reflects on or talks about memories that can stay fresh for days or months. And each reflection will bring something new, something we did not notice during the performance.

---

27 It is important to note that we always reflect upon moments of our past within the context of our present. And this always alters our memories. However, strong original emotions minimise permanent alternations.

28 Although rare, cases of hyperlexia indicate that our literacy could be partly imprinted in our genome.

29 I think that stage actors are wonderful practitioners of the Know Thyself Discipline. Stage acting theory and method offer a very good introduction.

Shakespeare taught this to our scientists, but they have not yet learned this part of the story – to tell their stories artfully and to tell more with less.

We have plenty to learn from the masters of emotions (artists) before we can start acting more credibly in our daily world. And, yes, there is much more bad acting outside the theatre than in it. Truly great stage acting does not lie. All emotions, thoughts and acts are in harmony. We cannot say this for our everyday thoughts and acts.

THE FRESH EMOTIONS OF OTHERS will evoke similar emotions in us. And if we once cut our finger, seeing someone else cut his will trigger a similar metabolic change in us.[30] Our emotions in tune with the emotions of others, is what we call empathy. And our emotions, not our words, spread our fresh memories (stories) throughout our culture. We talk about our fresh memories still laden with our emotions. And we listen to fresh memories of others, loading them with similar emotions of our own.

When these fresh memories are mostly about a familiar topic, newness is largely hidden. We are even able to silently speak together with the storyteller.[31] We will occasionally silently utter different words than the storyteller uttered, for we simply intended to hear a different word. And if the difference strikes us, our hearing falls into disarray. The only action we can then take is to stop the storyteller and establish a new starting point for talking together. The same is happening when we read…

Stories that are less familiar will prompt us to ask questions and ask for clarifications (repetitions) more often. The same is true about reading when we frequently go back to parts of the text we did not grasp properly before.

Entirely new stories to us — like learning a new dance, for example — raise the stakes dramatically. Here, empathy helps us to set up modified intents for unfamiliar actions, thoughts or feelings. These modified intents, derived from old stories, will still trigger old stories of ours. Fortunately, the veto criteria of modified intent remain intact.

*   *   *

Our consciousness frequently vetoes our old stories trying to modify them, just like we try to change our steps in the new dance. Our performance is halting, but our old stories start to change. And the same is happening when we study entirely new topics. We always need a lot of repetition for a fresh memory to sink in and become our new story.[32]

---

30 Seeing ourselves as others would see us (consciousness) may hold the key to what we would see and feel in the shoes of others (empathy).

31 This can be tested by measuring the tension of vocal cords while listening to a story. However, the story must be told directly by a storyteller to enable interactions with subjects. Subjects should be instructed to ask questions whenever something in the story is not clear.

32 The textbooks given to students are emotionally dry – hence the need for boring repetition. Text books laden with emotions and humour – text books that artfully tell more with less and can be read with interest many times – would greatly improve our educational practices.

A potential new story does not gain weight through repetition only. Fuelled by emotional charge, the engine of new stories will repeat them on its own. This is why we must try to artfully tell more with less...

Empathy is a powerful addition to the emotional charge of our fresh memories of the open eyes universe of a moment ago. Empathy revitalises our old stories through cultural means by reinitiating reconciliation cycles with other stories of ours.

Empathy is the glue that keeps us together in our culture.

WHAT DO YOU MAKE OF these eight lines on the left? Is it a transparent pyramid viewed from above or from below? Can you see both pyramids at the same time?

We can learn a lot about how we see from such ambiguous images. And no matter what, we cannot see all of the contradicting symbols at the same time. We need intent to see an alternative. And there is a delay until we actually see the alternative. And the delay is – at least — half a second. Rings a bell, doesn't it?

I read Dr. Benjamin Libet's book on a series of experiments he conducted that are now commonly known as "a half a second delay of our consciousness." He discovered that we become conscious of an urge to lift a finger half a second after neural activity necessary to lift a finger started. As many others were, I was speechless. If our consciousness does not initiate neural activity (decision), what does? Intrigued, I decided to perform an introspective experiment in, what I call now, the Know Thyself Discipline.

Although I did not have all of the equipment, I was able to replicate the subjective part of the experiment[33]. When I was motionless and without intent to move, there were only involuntary movements. Only when I intended to move was I able to detect the appearance of an urge to move in my consciousness. Libet's interpretation of data obviously needed a reinterpretation in the light of this introspective discovery. Moreover, intent shed new light on how we see, act, think and learn, etc.

*   *   *

Our intent can be attached to almost every story of our closed eyes universe. But attaching intent to a story is a story in itself. And as a story that often does not resemble our emotionally charged memories, it has to be repeated – or exercised. This is just like when I learned to use a new set of keys in a flawless and orderly manner. Now my fingers select the right key for the right lock on their own.

---

33 Just like with opening and closing your eyes – I encourage you to perform introspective experiments yourself. Introspective experiments, firmly based on scientific findings about us, will offer more complete answers about us than scientists alone can offer with their current approach from outside us. When scientists accept the reality of subjectivity they will have to accept the introspective method as a valid scientific method.

A story to sit down to study needs to have an intent that will preset veto criteria for our consciousness to weed out unrelated thoughts. And we instil this intent into our kids by our vetoes from outside for them. Here in Australia we instil intent into our kids to look right first when crossing the street. In Europe "look left" is instilled into the kids for the same situation.

The better we weave our webs of intents the better our performance will be. And the more we know (more precise stories about) a territory or a topic, the better we will weave our webs of intents – and perform flawlessly. This is an interesting dynamic between the intents and vetoes of our consciousness with a half a second delay[34]...

---

34 When we are buying a new car, for example, our non-consciousness generates a web of intents about the car to buy – long before we start to ponder it consciously. And our conscious pondering while facing the salesman is likely to produce a less satisfying result than our non-consciously generated web of intents. It is therefore much better to consciously ponder before we face the salesman and face him with much better knowledge of what we actually want.

DR. BENJAMIN LIBET STIRRED UPHEAVAL with his findings and their interpretation.[36] Even nanotubes were suggested to transport information back in time, and give us back our free will. Do we have free will then?

Of course we do! Libet established the first component – veto power of our consciousness. We can veto our thoughts, speech or actions. This may result in halting performance, but it will result in better stories eventually. To this, we only need to add the second component – intent.

With intent we can tease out our wanted old stories. Intent also presets criteria for our consciousness for what to veto or not to veto. Knowing this we can now get on my story about free will. I'll write and you read. Both are our habits — stories or sketchy images as far as our brain is concerned.

We may have strong intent (a wish) to go to the movies and when the time is right, our non-consciousness makes the decision.[37] But this decision might be contrary to a conflicting intent to study, for example. Conflicting intents need to be resolved and we ponder. And if a persuasive friend of ours adds her weight to the "go to the movies" intent, the "go to the movies" intent will prevail.

*   *   *

We cue a web of (habitual) intents that will initiate habitual actions — actions that will ultimately take us to a movie theatre. Since the "go to the movies" intent passed unchallenged, these intended actions are unlikely to be vetoed. And we will act flawlessly. The "go to the movies" intent initiates non-conscious decisions to check theatre locations and session times. The intent to walk can be here changed into take a bus, if another theatre has more suitable session times. As we go, we amend this web of intents on the fly – well before time for their execution comes. If the footpath is blocked, the intended web of intents will be amended to go around. And we might not even notice this. In fact, we might be free of deliberating so much that we will be able to think

---

35   This story alters Libet's. Note also that intent removes the ambiguity of Libet's findings that caused so much confusion in legal circles.

36   In fact, Libet based his research on findings in another research done by Hans H. Kornhuber and Lüder Deecke. In 1929, they found that a deliberate move requires 0.8 seconds of brain activity in average. They called this activity a Bereitschaftspotential, or readiness potential. The recorded readiness potentials were in some cases of up to 1.5 seconds.

37   This story is about our "free will"; our decision on any goal. This story can be easily modified into how we perform at work, think on a familiar topic, etc. Similar modifications can be done in other stories also.

or talk about something entirely unrelated. This is how our web of intents nudges us flawlessly to the theatre.

Our free will depends on how far ahead we can weave our webs of intents. Our free will also depends on how precise our mind map stories are.

UNFAMILIAR TERRITORY[38] CANNOT PROVIDE ANYTHING precise from a nonexistent mental map. The only help might be stories of others who knew the unfamiliar territory better than us. We ask for directions and land marks, and we go as directed intending to see landmarks and noticing very little else. We have to revisit or dream about the same place many times until we weave a detailed story about it.

Fortunately, our free will is only hampered by unknown territory that requires cognition rather than re-cognition. It still can take us to movies, but not flawlessly. There are, though, enemies to our free will. Firstly there are our individual habits (stories) that are central to many other stories of ours, like smoking or eating habits. For me, smoking is a ritual upon which I based my thinking and some other skills (stories or habits). If I stop smoking now, all the other stories of mine will be challenged for a very long time.

But the biggest obstacles to our free will are not in our personal habits. They are in our core cultural stories around which most of our other stories and stories of others are woven.

One of such core stories is the picture of a cause and effect driven universe, like a clock devised and put into motion by God (or the Big Bang). Our scientists, but not only them, have woven their stories around this core story since the 17th Century. Many generations weaved their stories around this story since. And now we have a simply staggering multitude of old stories endlessly repeated through centuries…

*   *   *

And then comes a lunatic like me and proposes that we dump this old story of ours.[39] "It's not working and we can have a better story with more explanatory power," says this barbarian in me. Hmm, I can only imagine heads spinning — especially the heads of people who consider themselves to be well educated. And our education **is** still based upon asking old questions and giving old answers…

Our free will is entirely powerless here, but the challenge of the new story will bore its way slowly into the depths of our stories. We will have different dreams probing the new story. And we will pause for a moment to test which of these two competing stories better reflects what we experienced a moment ago. But an awful lot of stories are in question, and going through them will take an awful lot of time. And until our

---

38   Unfamiliar topic, different working environment etc.
39   See Cause and Effect story.

old (modified) stories start to click together in a new way, we will be silent. But by then it could be too late…

To challenge our old core stories we need something much more powerful than our free will – we need our creativity and our open, wide-open eyes universe. And we need a lot of courage for leaps of faith in challenging our old core stories. Such leaps of faith are not even to be watched by fainthearted spectators… (Shut your eyes, please.)

OUR FRESH MEMORIES ARE IMPRESSED in us in many ways, but there are only two distinctive sources: sensations of our open eyes world and fresh memories of others. In the previous stories we outlined how our fresh memories sink in. And now we can look into how we weave them into our stories (habits).

Every fresh memory is emotionally charged.[40] And every fresh memory follows the same path towards becoming our new story. Almost immediately after a fresh memory is formed, non-conscious reconciliations with our other stories start. During the rest of the day, every free bit of our non-consciousness is used to compare, relate, re-evaluate… In progress, an unconfirmed fresh memory with a low emotional charge might lose its charge and be forgotten. But it also may receive a longer lasting weight from old stories of ours. And our fresh memories gain weight through confirmations and repetitions.

Our sleep frees additional resources in our brain. While we sleep we can reconcile our fresh memories with many more of our stories than we could while awake. Moreover, our brain activity that initiates physical action is inhibited and we are free to rehearse, probe and test. We improvise on a theme, like jazz players do, and find even better ways to act, feel or think in a novel way. As we dream we may even find solutions to problems we could not solve while awake. But, most importantly, we constantly come back to our fresh memories. In other words, we improvise and repeat to create a story for our non-consciousness. Such a story (habit) can be invoked (intended) in the future in an instant to act or think flawlessly in the new way.

*   *   *

However, our fresh memories do not necessarily lose their charge after a single good night's sleep. They may stay fresh for a while. Furthermore, fresh memories arisen from very large metabolic changes in us will always return to us to reflect upon in the few moments of our now. They will also be dreamed about, challenging ever widening circles of our old stories. Such memories/stories become an integral part of us until another fresh memory, arisen from large metabolic changes, challenges them.

As we share our stories with others they may gain a life of their own, just like Galileo's or Kepler's stories live among us today. And Galileo and Kepler still live among us through their stories…

---

40   The only other way we can wave a new story is through tedious repetition. The repetition can give weight to a new story to survive reconciliation cycles with other stories.

However, our closed eyes world, our old stories, prevails sometimes over our open eyes world. We forget the newness of every moment of our lives. And every new tree becomes the same old tree. Every new woman becomes the same as all other women. We start to live in a world without newness. Everything is boring – predictable — just like in our old story about the cause and effect driven universe… And we start to live in the hell of our own making…

Intent is of particular importance for what we call clear thinking. Our intent to think about a particular topic presets vetoing criteria for any other topic. This, with practice, enables us to focus — i.e. to foster occurrences of preselected topic-related thoughts only.

The narrow focus enables slow and deliberate re-evaluation of each thought as it occurs. And the smaller number of occurring thoughts enables much tighter re-evaluation of each in relation to others.[41]

Depending on our thinking skills, the results will vary. But they will always result in stories closer knit together — i.e. more differences between stories being reconciled. And presenting them to others to think through will subject them to similar processes, resulting in stories knit together even tighter.

We must be aware, though, that there is that hidden danger in the intent still present. We can intend only known (habitual) thoughts. Presenting our tightly knit stories only to people who think similarly will always produce much of the same. This is particularly dangerous in the sciences – disciplines ran away from each other too far. We must always widen our circles…

Without intents our thoughts wander. This brings fresh memories or a story that preoccupies us with a much wider spectrum of related stories. This is mostly done non-consciously. Very few of the possible conflicts will filter to our consciousness and be marked for further focused reconciliation. This "marking" is just another form of intent we can practice.

The number of these focus-defocus cycles will depend on how much importance we give to our intent to seek consistencies between stories. And with each cycle consistencies between our stories will grow.

---

41   In other words, we eliminate some of the shovels and chickens.

We cannot walk when we are born. This knowledge has not been transferred to us by our genome. Different kinds of knowledge had to be transferred to us through our genome instead. This makes us different from a calf, for example, that makes wobbly steps shortly after birth. Knowledge transfer through genes was augmented by knowledge transfer by cultural means. And our culture has a much longer memory than any individual...

Inevitably, how we, as individuals, come to existence must take two complementary components into account: genome and culture. Both of these components carry parts of the same or similar stories. Through genome we inherit partial stories of both of our parents. And from the moment of our birth we start to add missing parts — by cultural means. Our parents talk and play with us. We learn that a shape is a cube or pyramid. And no effort is spared to complete our inherited, partial stories with stories of culture we are growing into. And as we are growing up we also add our own stories.

Guided by our parents and teachers (external intents and vetoes), we evolve into social beings. Our desperate clinging to our toys gradually gives way to sharing – and we start to see ourselves as others would see us. We start to empathise with others, and share our stories with our peers in school. And we start to form a little culture of our own with our peers – a culture our parents cannot fully understand. And so we prepare ourselves to become the new generation.

Inevitably, we drown our individuality in the culture of our peers. We want to be like them in every possible aspect – but we also yearn for our lost individuality. We yearn to be "special" again, and we start to search for ourselves with the ultimate goal of knowing ourselves.

To really become mature we need to shed illusions about ourselves and the world around us. Being scientific here could help enormously.

THE 17ᵀᴴ CENTURY ESTABLISHED ANOTHER core story of ours – our reasoning faculties. We analysed our reasoning faculties to derive "rules" that are driving them. And we spelled them out in a variety of logics. And we banned emotions and humour from these rules. And with confidence, at the beginning of 20th Century, we were proclaiming that everything can be proven (explained) by logic and math…

Kurt Gödel did not agree. And he produced mathematical proof that everything cannot be proven (explained) by logic or math – turning debates into circular arguments. The funny thing is, we haven't noticed that yet. We construct computer models of the cause and effect driven universe. And only when we mathematically add causality our models start to "work". We have proven causality.[42] Similar models blew up into Wall Street's face and the global financial crisis is in the making now.[43]

Now if this is not a "shovel-chicken" story – I do not know what is…

Dry logic and math combined with Descartes' input → processing → output story reached their limits. The more we drive them the more they will blow up into our faces. The more we hide behind our iron curtains the more our theories of everything will be theories of nothing. Only open, wide open eyes and our creativity can give us back what we lost in our old stories (theories). Only when we say that we do not know, we can start to learn…

*   *   *

And we need to artfully tell more with less, and our stories will have then their echoes. With as high as possible emotional charge they can reach someone who can tell us that there are shovels and chickens in our story (theory). And we will clean up the chicken shed better…

Our reasoning (and intuition) cannot be imprisoned by rules. We need to free our reasoning faculties and let them evolve. Our reasoning was mummified for far too long.

---

42   This story was published almost everywhere – and it still makes me laugh.
43   Not yet clear solution at the horizon of 28 September 2008.

I WAS FACING THE BLANK stares of students when I talked from books about truth. I needed an introduction that would dispel these blank stares. I had to explore the question of truth from my own experiences. Do our experiences tell that we can give a meaning to something out there as we want to? Only a credible answer could explain to students how we can give whichever meaning we wish, to existence or non-existence of electrical current in a computer chip. But – I did not have a credible answer. My knowledge about truth was bookworm's knowledge without personal experiences behind. Writing paper on logic gates became a nightmare...

Then came a thought that loosened the grip of my bookworm's story about truth – fortune telling. Here we can assign a variety of meanings to the same phenomenon. But, what about other phenomena? It either rains or it doesn't rain. Can there be something else?

Obviously, I was not quite there yet and I was stuck for days. For some reason, not yet known to me, my thoughts often "digressed" to evolution, about which I was reading a book at the time. And then it struck me. The new story about truth felt like a physical shiver throughout my body.

As we evolved we were evolving our truths, our stories about everything around us. And we shared our truths. And when "it rains" did not match our fresh memories of a moment ago, we would say it's false. And when "it rains" matched our fresh memories, we would say it's true. If a phenomenon out there were important to us and if it were right in the middle, we would invent a new symbol. And with the new symbol we would be able to say, for example: It neither rains nor it doesn't; it hazes.[45]

*   *   *

This realisation enabled me to finish the paper in a couple of hours. However, my hopes to dispel blank stares were shattered. The blank stares of students were not dispelled. Even long pauses of my mentors filled with thoughts did not indicate an agreement at the horizon. I realised that the challenge of my new story is far greater

---

44   This story may draw blank stares – it is simply too contra intuitive for many. I would suggest reading it again after evolution and history parts are completed.

45   In simple terms, truth is affirmation of an old story of ours. However, there is always a clutter of shovels and chickens we tolerate or do not notice. There is, therefore, a need for another kind of truth that eliminates some of the clutter...

than I imagined. Practically all of my old stories were challenged. It took me decades to amend them so that they can make sense together – again.

This, making sense together is truth, all truth and nothing but the truth about the truth.

The truth is in our new and challenged stories clicking together in a new and beautiful way. The truth is in stories of our culture clicking together in a new and beautiful way. And each successful challenge will give new emotional charge to our new story. And each successful new story, carried by its emotional charge, will spread in our culture challenging other stories and transforming our culture.

The truth is real information. And the truth is creative and beautiful in harmony within and between all of our stories…

Some people believe in a myth – absolute truth, The Absolute Truth to be precise. This myth arose in the second century during political fighting between Christian traditions. (Old despots had some decency to proclaim themselves as just one god among others.) Christianity had a variety of traditions then and each of them wanted to be right. And what would be a better weapon than absolute truth? Owners of such a weapon are ultimate judges in who is right and who is wrong. The dogma[47] was born…

Philosophers and scientists also succumbed to the power grabbing lure of absolute truth, in history and nowadays. There was a very long period of belief in physical constants as a kind of absolute truth. And although there are enough doubts cast at constancy of constants (dogma), there are still many who believe in this myth.[48]

If it were not sad, it would be hilarious to see where the myth about absolute truth led us to – nihilism. The typical cry of nihilists is: "We will never know anything for certain!" (Read "certain" as "absolute truth".) They intuitively realised that there is no absolute truth. And this is the source of their desperation…

This story cannot be tested. This story is rather a challenge to those who still search for absolute truths, constants, hidden causes etc. This is the challenge to produce a single piece of firm evidence for any truth that will stay unchanged forever. This story is also a challenge to all our old stories based upon such concepts.

---

46 In the name of The Absolute Truth we killed and destroyed numerous cultures, even civilisations. And nowadays, seeing ourselves as others would see us (a picture of us from outside) helps suicide bombers feel "safe", for only this "us" within the picture will die.

47 In the 4th century, Constantine added his imperial weight to what should be and what shouldn't be in the Bible.

48 It seems that the joy of a discovery is sometimes spoiled by fears of having ones career burned at stake by peers. Radical ideas seem to be left to those whose stature can withstand the cyclones of criticism…

THE PICTURE OF US – how we see, feel, think and act – makes the notion of objectivity untenable. We inherited, through our genome, partial sketches (stories) of our brains. We completed them and sketched new ones in our brains as we grew into our culture. And we are sketching our own sketches every moment of our lives. And what we now see is inevitably biased towards our sketches (stories).

Knowing this, the meaning of being objective has to change. It is now obvious that we will never be able to see things of our open eyes universe as they are.[49] The "objectivity" rug has been pulled while we were standing on it. The only way we can regain our balance is to say that being objective is a "sum" of our subjectivities. But this "sum" is not a simple math…

You say chicken and I say shovel. Together we tell a story with a shovel and a chicken in it. We ask subjects about what they feel, but we refuse to fully embrace subjectivity. We are full of such contradictions. Others are also full of such contradictions. And contradictions between us make "summing up" a really messy business. But this mess is relatively tidy when we are within physicists' or biologists' culture only. Crossing the border between such cultures will expose an even bigger mess of shovels and chickens. And there is little hope for uniting them into a single culture soon.

But we have no choice but to start "summing up". Only "summing up" can restore some credibility to our claims of being objective.

---

49   Whenever we have our eyes open, we do not only see infinity, we also cognise or re-cognise at the same time. And this means the mapping of infinity with sketches of our brain. And we "lose" almost all of the differences.

A HABIT BREAKING EXERCISE IS our first step on the path towards our creativity. To break a habitual story, we need to create circumstances that will make the habitual story ridiculous. We can start with small challenges – "look at the left wrist to see the time." This story can be challenged by putting our time piece on the right. Just count your "oops" during the day…

Successes of such small challenges shake up the dust from other old stories of ours, making challenges easier. And we have so many small habits we can make ourselves look ridiculous for years to come. Each new small habit broken will create new ripples of non-conscious reconciliations. Each new small habit broken will add its bit to our dreams and we will improvise like jazz players do. And our ability to notice little things[50] will flourish. Little things will get higher emotional charges and they will be probed in our non-consciousness.

Habit breaking exercises will sensitise us to details – raising our levels of alertness. So prepared we need to expose ourselves to the open eyes world. Even to the theoretical physicist the source of data is our open eyes world.[51] An easy meandering stroll to the beach, for example, will reap rewards of our new levels of alertness. Our non-consciousness will be soaked with emotionally charged details in need of reconciliation. Only occasionally a thought will occur in our consciousness to be marked (intent) for a closer inspection later. And when I, for example, reach the beach[52], I sit outside a quiet coffee shop, sip an espresso and get busy with the marked thoughts I collected during the stroll.

*   *   *

Little things, or anomalies, have a wonderful power to blow our old theories apart. And even better, they blow them apart with outlines of new, emotionally charged fresh memory we will throw into cycles of reconciling. And the more metabolic changes we experience the wider the ripples will be. We will be hooked. We made the first step on the only path towards the theory of everything – our creativity.

---

50   They are called anomalies in the science.
51   Unfortunately, they shuttle too much between their labs (a tiny fraction of the open eyes world) and their models. An open, wide open eyes strategy may be better. Maybe we can then see entanglement in a flower.
52   Maroubra beach in my case.

If the God[53] particle cannot be seen in that little flower growing from the old fence wall, it will not lead us to a theory of everything – it will rather lead us to a theory of nothing…

Another, very special tool that can increase our creativity deserves a separate story.

---

53   Theoretically conceived, the God particle is supposed to give mass to all other particles. Actually finding it would resolve most of the problems quantum physics is facing. Among other things it should answer why we cannot walk through walls. Interestingly, the God particle was conceived on a stroll.

A TRIBE OF NATIVE AMERICANS, as usual, visited their shaman to tell them what kind of winter lies ahead. He tossed his bones and studied them. Finally he said: "It will be a long and harsh winter." And the whole tribe went over the mountain to gather wood for the harsh winter. But winter turned out to be mild and the tribe got cross.

Next fall, the tribe visited the shaman again. Uncomfortable, the shaman made the same prediction. A bit worried, he went to the meteorological office in the town nearby. Shyly he asked a meteorologist what kind of winter he thought was ahead. And the meteorologist said: "It will be a long and harsh winter." When questioned how he knew that, he took the shaman to the window and gave him binoculars. "Do you see that tribe on the mountain gathering wood? Well, that is how I know."

I hope that this old joke will be new to most readers. And I like old jokes that make me think. And I remember jokes that make me think. I like all forms of humour that made me think. And many of my stories here could have been written in humorous ways – but I chickened out. Humour can sometimes generate more hate than laughter.

Humour can generate a cognitive shift. Scientists themselves investigated the impact of humour and came up with this conclusion. As yet, scientists do not realise how powerful humour can be in presenting their research. As yet, scientists do not realise that a ridiculous perspective of their research can generate a cognitive shift in them also.

But this tool that can help us to be more creative requires a sense of humour.

We often say that our kids are our future. But knowing how we teach our children makes our future look grim. We ask our kids to ask questions we already asked before and give answers we already gave before. But we do not let our kids ask questions and give answers we did not think of before. Our schools sterilize our children of all creativity, rare good examples excluded…

In an attempt to help teachers we introduced tests to "objectively" grade our kids. We even "objectively" measure intelligence quotient (IQ). But is the asking old questions and giving old answers a sign of intelligence?

Tests ask of our kids old questions and demand old answers. IQ tests only indicate how well we have structured old stories of our culture. And they could be pretty offensive to kids of other cultures. This is what happens when we try to introduce "objectivity" into our schools – we forget the most important part – to teach our children to think on their own. And teachers became more interested in their own wellbeing than in kids'.

Teachers must relearn the art of helping their students to articulate questions nobody has asked before. They also need to help our kids to articulate answers nobody has given before.

Our kids need habit breaking exercises. Our kids need funny perspectives, even at an early age. Our kids need to learn how to challenge everything they are taught in school. And our teachers need to learn to loosen up. Even the most ridiculous views will reinforce the lesson – if the lesson can survive the onslaught, though. And we need to learn to trust such teachers. Only such an approach can prevent turning our kids into tired clones of ourselves…

BEFORE WE TRY TO ANSWER the question about what is information, we have to shatter gigantic misinformation about what is information.

Claude Shannon measured information entropy. He worked for Bell laboratories (telegraphs and telephones then). He knew that, in the real world, messages are never encoded without errors – entropy. And he calculated how much redundancy must be in a message to neutralize the most of possible errors.

And then cometh hatching of an industry from The Duck's egg.[54] Shannon's entropy was turned into information – entropy (chaos) became order by reversing a sign in Shannon's equations. The greatest ever blunder, in my opinion.[55]

Now we have a huge industry in which professionals do not know what they are talking about. And some of those professionals call themselves – scientists. What they do not know and still talk about is: information.[56] Other scientists also fell into the trap of this false story while the general public uncritically accepted the story. Nowadays we have the Internet cluttered with such "information". And this clutter contains contradictions as a rule rather than as an exception. This is not information. This is information entropy.

A new version of a story we already know cannot be information. A new story confirming our old stories may be an addition, but not information. Only a story that challenges our old stories can be informative. If we believe that the Earth is flat, a new story that it is round can be informative. If we believe that our sun is circling around the Earth, a new story that it is the other way around can be informative.

---

54   See The 18th Century – The Duck.

55   If there are bigger ones, I'll be glad to hear about them.

56   The existing computers process patterns – not information. The distinction can be seen in Etruscan inscriptions. The inscriptions are obviously regular patterns. But we do not have a clue what they tell, i.e. we do not know what they mean (information). The inscriptions mean nothing to us and the fact that they meant something to somebody once upon a time is irrelevant.

A FRESH MEMORY OF A new story we receive has the potential to become information only if it is at odds with some other stories of ours.[58] Even then its potential does not necessarily translate into information. A heard story can be forgotten as soon its emotional charge evaporates.

The potential of a heard story is starting to be realised as we connect the dots. Each dot is a resolved conflict between two stories. But connecting dots needs time since we do not connect all of the dots easily. And, in progress, the new story may lose its emotional charge, diminishing the challenge to other old stories of ours.

The value of potential information could be calculated from how many other stories are challenged by a new story. And this is in itself individual. At the end, the realised potential will also vary from person to person. And this highlights the importance of how we inform, i.e. tell our stories. On the receiving end, a weight loss regime of habit breaking exercise will ease connecting the dots...

Introspectively, it will be impossible to estimate how many of our old stories were changed, dropped or replaced. Most of these changes are done non-consciously or while dreaming.

However, since we are talking about our closed eyes world, with a rough subset of stories of our culture, we can start constructing a model. Simulations will give us further insights. Comparing these insights with real people will give us ideas to further improve our models. Through our models we could also arrive at another measure of information — a measure that will reflect how much the volume of the data in the model shrank when the new story was integrated.

*   *   *

Thomas Kuhn was right when he said that niggling anomalies give rise to (scientific) revolution. What he probably did not know is that we all have such small revolutions we call information. And we all can deliberately challenge huge numbers of our old stories. We all can imagine, construct a credible story, think and wait...[59]

---

57   This story of mine is altered Kolmogorov's.
58   The process of internalising a new story (told by others) is exactly the same as internalising other fresh memories of our experiences in our open eyes world.
59   Imagination is our most potent tool for constructing hypotheses with potential to clean up our chicken sheds.

MY PREVIOUS STORIES OUTLINED THE theory for the Know Thyself Discipline. These outlines can be now used to articulate Know Thyself Theory as a more comprehensive story.

The Know Thyself Discipline recognises our open eyes world as an infinite universe full of unique phenomena that are only reflected by our stories in our limited closed eyes universe. The dynamics between the two defines how we see, think and act in any of them and how unique phenomena are reflected in our stories.

However, not all of our stories are active in every moment of our lives. We do not expect sensations related to all of them every moment. We need, therefore, to preselect a likely subset of our stories based upon fresh memories and confirmed stories of the previous moment. This is much more economical and our seeing, thinking and acting can be executed much faster. The basic concept of the Know Thyself Discipline can now be outlined as dynamic terplay between these three components:

$$[\text{sensations}] \leftrightarrow [\text{theory/hypothesis}] \leftrightarrow [\text{stories/habits}]$$

Our theory/hypothesis is basically a web of intents that govern our feeling, seeing, thinking or acting. All is well when everything goes as planned. However, when sensations do not match our intents, our seeing, thinking or acting falls into disarray. Results of failure have to reach our consciousness. Failed intents will point at old stories we guessed wrongly. Strong sensations will indicate at intents we failed to raise. And the time of recovery will depend on the number of failures…

* * *

Strength of sensations or number of failures is translated into an emotional charge for our fresh memories and another process is triggered within us – the fight for survival between our fresh memories (potential stories) and our old stories. This fight renews our closed eyes universe and we become better equipped to form better theories in future moments of our lives.

We can now use this knowledge of how we feel, see, think and act to look into ways how to improve on our seeing, thinking and acting.

---

60 Psychologists are already practicing introspection, for there is no other way of interpreting their data. However, their introspective method is not well specified. I hope that this little story of mine will help here.

SCIENTISTS OBSERVE JUST LIKE OTHER people. They are a bit more methodical in observing, though. Know thyself theory can easily be adapted to describe scientific observation:

$$[\text{sensations}] \leftrightarrow [\text{hypothesis}] \leftrightarrow [\text{theories/stories/habits}]$$

As in the Know Thyself Discipline, the first danger is in intents (expectations). Intents are derived from the hypothesis and our observations (interpreted sensations) will be less challenging to our hypothesis. Measurements are here critical to detect every possible anomaly. And there will be anomalies – always…

Unfortunately, we too often dismiss these anomalies as errors in measurements – another name for that little devil that spoils an otherwise perfectly predictable outcome. If there are anomalies we need to observe more to rule out errors as much as possible. For only anomalies can give us inkling on how our sensations (raw data) were altered into observations (perceived data).

We often say that we overcame this problem with very precise equipment. Think again… Our equipment measures a very narrow spectrum of our sensations or what might be our sensations. Our equipment is built to be biased.

The second major problem is in dissonance between our theories (stories) we choose to test. Some disciplines diverged too much, becoming separate sciences[61]. And theories of one are too often completely useless in another. And observations in one are completely useless in another. Our observations and our theories became biased towards our own little disciplines…

The third major problem is our tendency to observe a phenomenon in isolation from other phenomena. This could be partially justified when we can experience the phenomenon directly, since we can distinguish between properties of the phenomenon and properties emerging from its interplays with other phenomena. In quantum physics, however, we are on a very slippery slope, deriving properties of wavicles (**wav**es-par**ticles**) from interplays between wavicles. And we saw that we cannot derive emergent properties from properties of system's constituent parts…

---

61 Note that we stopped speaking about science and disciplines within it. We are now talking about entirely different sciences with their own rules and criteria.

THE PICTURE OF A CAUSE and effect driven universe was in trouble. We could not predict or replicate anything entirely. So we added to this picture a little devil that spoils an otherwise perfectly predictable outcome – chance. We could now gloss over all anomalies whenever we wanted to. We could now point at all anomalies whenever we wanted to. And sceptics caught the flu…

We stopped asking for more observations whenever "the evidence was inconclusive". Instead we established criteria for what are good, not very good and naughty, naughty observations. The sceptics' mild rebuke, "the evidence is inconclusive", reveals how they slipped into such bias. Such rebukes imply that old stories sceptics are standing for **are conclusive**. In other words, there was very little room left for observing anomalies of our old stories (theories, data interpretations etc.) we accepted as true.

A mild rebuke threatens sometimes to turn into fury whenever a reputable scientist dares to look into anomalies of our basic old stories. The reputation of a reputable French chemist was furiously torn apart simply because he investigated claims of homeopaths. And a reputable scientific journal published his peer reviewed work with an unprecedented "foreword" or "disclaimer". Ugly! Did we start to censor or self-censor our observations?

The Know Thyself Discipline tells us that our perception is biased towards our old stories. Consequently, we have to fight our perceptual bias. Adding another bias on top of it only makes things worse.

*　*　*

Obviously, I'm disappointed with some "scientists" developing bookkeeper's culture and "cooking the books" along the way. These observations go into the good science account and these into the bad science account… And science is often done mechanically. We change something in our calculations and then seek specific data to confirm our calculations. And the Know Thyself Discipline tells us that we are likely to see what we expect to see…

I think that I am expressing the wishes of many about what science should be. I'm not so sure though that those many have a clear picture of what some "scientists" are turning into… Do we have guardians of old stories – guardians of Absolute Truth that will burn us at the stake?

PhD (philosophiae doctor) was once the highest title a scientist could earn. Philosophy was considered then as an umbrella for all other scientific disciplines. Then, there was science only. Then, there were no sciences – only scientific disciplines. Then, a candidate for the title had to articulate an original idea into a coherent thesis that can be defended in all disciplines. Then, the candidate had to defend his thesis demonstrating his knowledge in most of the disciplines. Then, there was no fairytale ending, for the candidate had to answer the last question: Is his thesis proven beyond any doubt? And then, only a negative answer will earn him the title…

These high standards for academics started to erode rapidly in late 19th century; to be completely turned to dust in the 20th. The title is now generously given not for original ideas, but rather for chewing over old ones – number crunching. And original ideas became dangerous, for they could spell the end to many assumptions built in the number crunching. Many years of "fruitful" number crunching could be simply wasted. And who would like his lifetime of "fruitful" number crunching wasted?

For many, the science is now about number crunching: "Do not think on your own, do your measurements as you are told and the glory of being called a scientist will be bestowed upon you. Do not let others to think on their own either! Especially, do not let them say what they think. If they try, shut them up. And if they do not shut up, let's excommunicate them."

For Galileo, excommunication would be life threatening. He could not afford to challenge Church and Inquisition. And they shut him up. There is no evidence for his "Eppur si muove" ("And yet it moves") remark, but he did demonstrate much more courage than we do today facing churches and inquisitions of number crunchers.

*   *   *

Science has been shattered and pieces (sciences) have been hijacked by number crunchers. "Ownership" is obtained and maintained by encrypting code – jargon nobody else will be able to understand. And this is evident in the increase of number of generations a new idea needs to be accepted (if it is not burned at the stake from very beginning).

There is no progress without a challenge to old beliefs (ideas, theories). This is especially true in science. There is no room in science for defenders of the faith – inquisitors. Crunching numbers is valuable and necessary in science and elsewhere, but it is not self justifiable. Crunching numbers is a tool only to test and verify ideas, including new ideas – no matter how heretical they might seem to number crunchers.

The use of religious terminology of our past (and present) is – deliberate.

DARWIN'S STORY STARTS WITH OBSERVED physical (anatomical) differences between similar species but in different habitats. There was only one possible explanation. The same species adapted themselves to different environments. In other words, they became different species through different physical changes.

Now we see evolution as series of sporadic bursts of physical changes in time. Only occasionally, there were dramatic changes that would put some species at a disadvantage and offer advantages to others. And we are growing and tending our evolutionary trees. But, are we overemphasising physical changes and giving genes only shaping powers?

I would say – yes. We are evolving every moment of our lives. Every moment of our life we create stories that reflect our environment.[62] This is our way of evolving that only sporadically needs a change in our bodies. We even change our genome without changing physical characteristics. And if we are to change physically in the future, this change will be driven by our stories.

And I would say that this is exactly the same with all other living organisms. Only sporadically their stories reflect such changes in their environment that make a physical change necessary.

Maybe we should add this subtle change to Darwin's story.

---

62   There is a major shift in research from genome to its expressions – epigenome. Epigenome of identical twins shows rapid changes as they grow older, indicating that the cumulative effect of the changes is likely to impact genome itself.

The know thyself theory is not only valid for us. It is
also applicable to life in general.

My little scientific stories reached the borderline where the interplay of our individual selves gives rise to our culture. This interplay can be found in all living organisms, from single cell organisms to us – humans. And this interplay has an impact and is reflected in stories on both sides of this, rather artificial, borderline. There is also another, rather artificial, borderline between our culture and our culture's living environment. Interplay of all these three components impacts and is reflected in stories of each of them. The fourth, also rather artificial, borderline between the living and non-living environment is implied only, but in our open eyes world we do have interplay between all four "components".

I would say that this is what defines life, although borders remain blurred. They should remain blurred in the same way we classify intelligence of other species. The more similar they are to us, the more likely we are to give them a higher IQ. (Maybe we need a different IQ tests for tomatoes, do we?)

Every living organism is unique and has to face its own equivalent of our open eyes universe. Even humble peas grafted from the same plant distinguish themselves from one another.[63] (Chemical signature was ruled out, but nothing else was offered as explanation. So much for musings of philosophers on identity issues…)

Just like us, every organism has to create its own stories for their own closed eyes universe. And just like us, it shares its stories with genetically similar organisms. In single cell organisms this sometimes means an exchange of genes. However, as stories about yeast indicate, there are other means of story exchanges. (Yeast cultures were found to be quite a noisy bunch. Yeast also demonstrated something like empathy.)

Exchanges of stories with genetically dissimilar organisms also occur. Sometimes we consider these exchanges destructive (cancer or a shark are good candidates). Sometimes we consider these exchanges constructive, as symbiosis is. In this, our human tendency to egoistically interpret what is constructive or destructive is dangerously destructive.

With such a perspective on life in general, we are much better equipped for explorations of the non-individual components of self. To do this we will add trends from our past to peek into the future with a few possible stories.

---

63   Dr. Omer Falik and Dr. Ariel Novoplansky found that two peas compete with their roots even when
    their genome is virtually the same. (90th Annual Meeting of the Ecological Society of America)

WE LIVED FOR A LONG time along the eastern coast of what is now South Africa. We did not migrate. Our culture was pretty much a seafood gathering culture. And there was plenty of seafood. And we may have invented a variety of ways to catch a fish. We may have also visited an island or two on a trunk of a tree… But we did not migrate.

Homo erectus and other cousins of ours migrated much earlier than us. And the changing environment may have given their cultures a push we experienced much later. And their semipermanent settlements may have solidified their new stories as ours will solidify our stories much later. Can you imagine better trackers for our culture? And our trackers were coming back with loads of new stories, some of them entirely incomprehensible to us for a very long time.

Whatever our story might have been we started our journey, meeting our ancestors on our way, and sharing stories with them. We did it carefully and slowly at the beginning to evolve our cognitive skills… Our cousins and our evolved cognitive skills may have made our migrations easier. There is only one point of possible contention. Did shared environments and shared stories induce genetic changes in some of our humanoid ancestors? This would mean a kind of evolutionary convergence…

Comparisons of us before our early migrations and us now strongly indicate how our early migrations evolved, enabling the emergence of our culture and our modern consciousness and civilisation later. I will, therefore, weave a few stories; interplaying components that helped us evolve into what we are now.

AS A SPECIES, WE EMERGED approximately a quarter of a million years ago. But we did not move much. There was no that familiar question in us: What is beyond that distant hill on the horizon? For more than hundred thousand years we just sat along the eastern coast of what is now South Africa. Physically we were Homo sapiens[64], but back then we were far, very far, from what we are now. It seems that we were then at the brink of being an evolutionary dead end…

Not much moving indicates that our sense of space and time was poor. Our cognition (not re-cognition) was probably dreadfully slow.[65] And to migrate we needed to have very fast cognition with a highly evolved sense of space and time. But, we were not moving and evolving our cognitive skills. What might have broken this vicious circle?

When we think about Homo sapiens we forget that our cousins were living among us. We did not invent making our stone tools from scratch. We learned these stories from our cousins. And they had their cultures and stories, if not spoken then signed and grunted. And we exchanged stories with them… Just like when we meet indigenous people who have never seen members of our culture.

Our cousins migrated even before we emerged. What triggered their migrations is anybody's guess, but their migrations were never a one-way road. Neither were ours. There was always someone turning back. Did their detailed stories trigger in us curiosity to see for ourselves what is beyond that distant hill on the horizon…?

Our best guess would be – yes. A steady, well-known environment always made us feel safer. Without a well-evolved sense of space and time our detailed stories (detailed sketches) prevented fast cognition. And the thought of moving to new, unknown territories may have been terrifying to early Homo sapiens. Only detailed stories about a new territory behind that hill on the horizon could dispel some of these fears. And only our returning cousins and the braver ones of us could tell us such detailed stories.

When we finally moved, we moved cautiously. But as our sense of space and time evolved we moved faster and faster — faster than our cousins. Our mental maps were

---

64 At this stage, we could not have been conscious in modern sense. However seeds of its modern aspects may have been present. For these seeds to grow and bear fruit we had to start our migrations, start building settlements and start seeing ourselves as others would see us – civility, civilisation with much stronger intent/veto mechanism. We also may have had a rudimentary culture based mostly on empathy. We lived in relatively small groups and to grow a group into a tribe, our culture had to evolve to tie much more individuals.

65 Maybe we were better than chimps today that re-cognise each other on the whole of the body basis. However, we were likely to still have very complex stories about each other and the rest of our environment – making our recognition slow and cognition even more so.

formed more quickly. Our details of anything were sketchier and sketchier, thus speeding up our cognition and re-cognition. And instead of re-cognition of the whole of a body our attention to details turned to the face. And the face is now how we cognise and re-cognise each other.

When we moved to new territory most of our old stories about our environment had to be replaced by new ones. But there were old stories of ours that did not have to be replaced. Even migrating for several generations did not change these old stories much. We, along with our culture, lifted our eyes towards our old stories that did not change.

Almost every morning the sun would rise. Almost every evening the sun would set. And even on cloudy days we knew that there was sun behind the clouds.

At night there was the moon – changing shape noticeably every day. And very quickly we were able to predict what shape it would take tonight. Our moon story was changing and yet remained the same. Our sense of cycles was born and the notion that our moon and sun are reflected in tides may have been conceived then.

Only our stories about stars seemed permanent – never changing. For far too many generations our ability to remember our stories about stars remained unchanged. There were only a few stars that were not fixed to our skies. And they required our attention.

Skies were unchanged wherever we moved. Stories about our skies could be told to our children wherever we were. And they could guide us wherever we were going.

Our stories about skies became core stories around which all other stories of our migrating culture revolved. Because we were entirely focused on stars even very small changes were noticed. A star would sink behind a horizon, but if we moved back it would reappear.

*   *   *

Millennia of migrations may have established a more complete picture of stars we see and stars beyond the horizon. Oral traditions are quite powerful in preserving our core stories. And we started to cross oceans. And seasons, we only intuited before, could be explained now. We probably thought that our seasons only reflected positions of our stars, and the notion that everything around us is just a reflection of skies was probably conceived then.

We made another few evolutionary steps towards what we are now…

WE LOVE OUR PARENTS. WE love our wives. We love our friends. And we love our children. But we lose them. And we lay the lost ones just like they were sleeping. With the fresh memory of the loss emotionally charged to the brim, we were constantly returning to our stories about lost ones. And we dreamed about our lost ones – awake — just like they were really only sleeping. And they stayed with us, as alive, for the rest of our lives. And this was probably true for Homo sapiens even before we migrated. We were probably also placing our dead at a place and visiting their resting place whenever our stories about them prompted us.

But when we started our long journeys, we could rarely go back to visit our lost ones. Seemingly, only stories about our lost ones travelled with us. It was nothing tangible. It was nothing you can see, hear or touch. But it was there with us. It would recur in our dreams as alive. It would recur here and now in an invisible world. We did not need to visit their bodies any more.

We were probably not materialists or atheists before we started our journeys. There were probably some spiritual elements before we started our journeys. But our spirit world broke almost all of the chains of the matter on our journeys…

OUR SPIRIT WORLD DID NOT break all of the chains though. Just telling about our lost ones to our young ones needed something tangible – something they could show to their young ones for stories to last over many generations.

Carrying items to represent our lost loved ones was, mildly said, impractical during our migrations. We would quickly break our backs under piles of such items. We had to look for something that was with us all the time, something we did not need to carry around. And we found this by looking up – into our sky.

The sun, moon, stars and patches of darkness between them were populated with our lost loved ones. And our lost loved ones became immortal and we could point at them while telling their stories to our young ones. And each story about our lost loved ones had to teach our young ones about the world that surrounded us.

Legions of stories of our lost loved ones could not survive over many generations. Only those that struck a chord in us could burn themselves into our memory and the memories of our young ones. As with us, they had to be emotionally charged and relevant in our open eyes world. And we started to learn to tell artfully more with less. Our stories grew more abstract and our skies turned into a magical world of myths…

Our long lost loved ones got powers beyond any human. And such powerful spirits demanded to be represented by equal power – the power of art.

And we made new steps towards what we are now…

OUR EARLY LANGUAGE WAS PROBABLY not much better than the grunts and postures of our cousins. And we were probably re-cognising others mostly through "whole of the body" complicated sketches in our mind – just like chimps of today[66]. Our poor sense of space and time without a clear sense of cycles simply did not allow for the sense of rhythm and melody we have now.

The speed of our early migrations offered space and time as a new structuring principle for our language. The speed of our cognition and re-cognition brought about simpler sketches for our utterances. And, with simpler sketches of our utterances we could start to weave our stories with rhythm and intonation. And fewer lines in our sketches also meant higher levels of abstraction.

With a fluent and melodic language we were able to weave tighter stories of ours. And fresh, sketchier memories were much easier to reconcile with our, also sketchier, old stories. And all this turned us into the keenest observers in the history of our planet. And the transfer of our accumulated knowledge shifted further away from our genes. The transfer of accumulated knowledge by cultural means had never been seen at such levels before.

Our fast evolving language really made the most of what we are now... Our tightly woven stories gave new strength to our culture that will allow for many more members – and our migrating groups grew into tribes.

---

66   Primatologists Frans de Waal and Jennifer Pokorny at Emory University in Atlanta looked into how chimps re-cognise. (Advanced Science Letters, DOI 10.1166/asl.2008.006)

Our improved sense of cycles, space and time gave us an unusual and powerful tool – so powerful that we could tell stories about our powerful old loved ones with the power they deserved. And we started to tell their stories with a rhythm. And we started to dance with the rhythm. And we chanted and we modulated our voices.

And our spirits were happy. And our already powerful spirits became even more powerful. And we felt their power — power that united us. And whenever we danced and chanted in unison, we felt a magical sense of togetherness – we would never feel so powerful otherwise. Our dances and chants lifted all of us to higher levels of understanding each other. And through our dances and chants our culture weaved us into a cloth of much more closely knit individuals. And the culture of much more closely knit individuals could hold together many more individuals.

Our culture grew in strength and numbers. And with numbers grew new ideas. The rhythm of our chants shaped our words as much our words shaped the rhythm. The rhythm became a tool in our language and our language evolved further.

And when rhythm could not give our chants more power, we started to modulate our voices. We also found various ways to invoke a chant of a moment ago – like rhyme for example. And we weaved our stories tighter and tighter together. And we learned how to tightly weave huge stories – like Homer's – that will define our civilisations.[67]

---

67   Homer was probably the single author of most of the Iliad and the Odyssey. His work may have reshaped some of much older stories into a contemporary story of 9th or 8th century BC. His poems were foundations for ancient Greek civilisation and they were considered as primary education for more than a millennium in Greek cultures and the Roman Empire. It should be noted, though, that Greek cultures (cities, colonies) never had as much of a sense of unity as cultures of other civilisations had.

Denis Dutton expressed similar view in his book "The Art Instinct" that is rather centred at storytelling.

THE PREVIOUS STORIES OUTLINED COMPONENTS that were critical in our evolution during early migrations and finally settling down into a civilisation. So bear them in mind until we reach the final destination – civilisation[68] and what we are now.

As we moved north along the coast of east Africa, we may have improved on the trunk of a tree to bypass obstacles on the land. This fixed our migration routes and we may have had a "follow that kelp[69]" rule – this was where we could catch fish...

The east coast of Asia and then west coast of America followed. Another route our culture took was along the coast of South East Asia to Australia and across the Pacific to numerous islands. The route to Europe was opened much later.[70]

This is our latest story about our early migration, but what does it have to do with our culture and us? Well, the constantly changing environment demanded new stories (cognition) all the time.[71] This was an extreme habit breaking exercise for our culture. Without strong old stories (re-cognition), our cultures were vulnerable. And with our vulnerable culture we were vulnerable too...

Settling for a while was a matter of survival. Thus, our culture learned to settle and move again. And we would settle and move again, without changing environment too much. It took only a few generations to form enough firm old stories and then move long distances again.

On our way, we likely met our cousins or others like us heading back or settled. And if a conflict was avoided we were likely eager to hear their stories. The importance of knowing what lies ahead must have been powerful motivation for cooperation. Our culture may have learned then the power of cooperation – the seed of our civilisations.

---

68 Not all of our cultures reached the final destination though. There are a few possible reasons for that. Environments like rainforest, for example, may have hindered growth in numbers of a culture.

69 It is interesting to note that many cultures along first migrational weaves still enjoy algae in their menus.

70 The out of Africa migrational wave into Europe probably did not evolve navigational skills similar to cross the Pacific wave.

71 Two groups of researchers came to this conclusion independently. By reading single-letter references they were able to tell someone with a Finnish heritage, Dane or German. They practically reproduced Europe's map. (Nature; DOI:10.1038/nature07331 & Current Biology; DOI:10.1016/j. cub.2008.07.049)

As we moved we had to be curious and creative. And our sense of space and time had to evolve rapidly.[72] Otherwise, we would be lost… Then born thirst for new discoveries (stories) drives us even today. Our early migrations made us truly human.

Shouldn't we thank all of our ancestors for helping us to evolve into what we are now?

---

72 Our sense of space and time may have been even keener then than today as some aborigine navigators demonstrated.

MANY TEMPORARY SETTLEMENTS FOR FEW generations only, gradually turned into few settlements only for many generations. Our stories about stars beyond the horizon may have lost their significance, but our stories of cycles and seasons did not. With seasons, we moved from one settlement to another. But during our migrations we developed a taste for new stories. Could we find new stories within little changing environments?

We already had domesticated animals as we moved from one seasonal settlement to another. And we were gathering seasonal berries, seeds, nuts etc. And then we would move to another to catch fish, for example. But some were better at catching fish than in gathering. And it was much easier to move fish or berries between settlements than to move the whole tribe. So gatherers chose to stay at the best place for gathering. Fishermen chose the best place for fishing. Gatherers learned how to improve their gathering while fishermen learned how to improve their catches. With our sense of seasons we started to look beyond the surface of our now well-known environments.

And we found new stories. Agriculture entirely removed the need to move between semipermanent settlements. And fishermen learned to catch and preserve enough fish for all. Only herders moved with the seasons. Digging beyond the surface for new stories did bring new stories virtually – metals. There was enough to explore and our semipermanent settlements became permanent.

Our culture established cooperation between now permanent settlements. And permanent settlements emerged giving rise to another important trait of our culture – sense of permanency. However, different settlements had different, now permanent, environments. And stories of these permanent settlements started to differ. Our culture heard alarm bells tolling. Members of the previously same culture did not fully understand each other anymore…

*   *   *

To survive, our culture needed something to unify these falling away parts. And this unifying force emerged from already existing stories woven in times of migrations and semipermanent settlements – religion and law[73]. A kind of polytheism empowered with permanency. Our stories were meant to last – forever.[74]

Stories meant to last forever also meant settlements to last forever. Building materials were carefully chosen to last forever. Constructions were carefully made to last forever.[75] Large numbers of permanent settlements also required careful management and keeping – records. And not knowing the full stories of other settlements demanded something to keep ourselves in check. Something that would make us look at ourselves as others would see us...

---

73   Religion and law were often inseparable in early civilisations since religion offered much needed ethics. However, during the life of a civilisation it became apparent that there are aspects of everyday life religious ethics and tribal traditions did not cover well enough. This emphasised a need for civil law to be spelled out. Combination of both often prescribed what needs to be intended and vetoed by our consciousness.

74   Vedas are traced back to at least ten thousand years BC. Oral traditions often preserved pronunciations and intonations so well; written traditions never could.

75   Long lasting buildings were long lasting stories themselves supporting the longevity of other stories of our cultures and civilisations. Civilisations that did not have long lasting buildings usually did not last long.

WHEN WE CLOSE OUR EYES we do not lose our consciousness. When we try to visualise, all we witness are sketchy images with degrees of vividness. These degrees of vividness in the closed eyes universe are induced by higher than usual activity of our closed eyes. And vividness can be practiced and improved. This closed eyes activity is similar to the rapid eye movement (REM) periods during our sleep. However, in both cases the intended sketches (stories) are triggers of what we will imagine or dream about. They are also called schemas or symbols and they are quite similar to a sketch of an apple – a minimum of lines required to recognise the apple. And these sketches are linked to other sketches – words or symbols we utter.

Symbols are what enter into our consciousness. Nothing else can enter into our consciousness. And symbols are what we use to share our stories. In civilisation, though, we need to control our urges, since we cannot fully understand each other as in our culture. And we resolved this need with a new perspective that made us see ourselves as others would see us – our modern consciousness. Seeing ourselves as others would see us is only one step away from feeling what others might have been experiencing – empathy. And empathy paved the way to intents[77] and vetos – intents to respect others and vetos for our disrespectful urges. We became civil to each other.

As with a developing child, this new story of ours needed to be repeated many times in many minds. And civility spread slowly through our cultures. But civility also fixed our old stories and imprisoned us within walls of old answers on old questions. With unchecked civility we planted the seed that could spell the end to our civilisation.

And our social aspect of consciousness started to rise and fall with our civilisations.

---

76 Rather a social aspect of consciousness as how would others see us or modern consciousness.
77 I suspect that socially related intents (veto criteria) were initially weak and vague – in need of generations of guidance – and religions may have played a major part here.

OUR EARLY CIVILISATIONS FELL. OUR not so ancient civilisations also fell. And our own civilisation is in danger of falling if we do not identify where the threat is coming from.

It is hidden in civilisation's nature – strive for permanency. At the beginning every civilisation had novel answers (stories) for novel situations. Thus, early creativity always made civilisations flourish.

But all this early creativity, barbaric in its nature, could not hold many cultures together. Only intents and vetoes of our consciousness could keep together many different cultures. And civility would re-establish the cycle of old answers on new questions. And our civility gave its stamp of approval. Our old answers became like a dam behind which novel situations accumulated like water.

Our old civilisations had only one chance to survive – to start asking questions nobody asked before and start giving answers nobody gave before. (Very uncivil towards old answers on old questions…) But this would be a new civilisation raised from the ashes of the old one. And for a suicide like this no civilisation was ready – and our old civilisations fell. Not all though, but did we learn the lesson from the surviving ones?[78]

Being civil to each other stifled criticism of each other… And this enabled endless repetitions of old stories (answers) for novel situations. Should we welcome barbarians as old Romans did[79]…?

---

78 Chinese and Indian civilisations demonstrated extraordinary vitality. Their historical openness to any religion might have been one of the keys to their survival. On the other hand, the religious intolerance might have an opposite effect. Strict religious stories that do not tolerate alternatives always lead to erosions in society, morality and mental integrity. And compromised ethics weakens our socially related intents and vetoes. This is well reflected in alarming levels of antisocial behaviour and lack of empathy nowadays.

79 There is a poem about one Roman city awaiting barbarians and being disappointed when they did not come…

WE INHERITED MANY STORIES FROM previous millenniums. This included stories of Old Rome. But we lost our inheritance (and social aspect of our consciousness) with the fall of the Roman Empire.[80] Islam was rapidly spreading by sword while Christianity was in retreat, losing the last of the inherited stories individuals may have preserved…

We were drifting around very much like our ancestors between semipermanent settlements. The only story we preserved was in a book – the Bible. But very few could read, even in the ranks of clergy. And as our warlords settled to become lords, clergy started to rule all the aspects of our lives the lords did not care to rule over. To very few there was something beyond that distant hill…

However, developing trade in the 10th Century started to take people beyond that distant hill. Crusades to check or reverse the spread of Islam took even more people beyond that distant hill. And although crusades brought dominance to neither, we did find a huge treasure – our old lost Roman stories in stories of shrunken Byzantine Empire and of Arabs. And we learned not only about Islam and Arabic science, but also about ancient Greek philosophies and Indian[81], rather than Arabic, numerals.

Protagoras' story "man is the measure of all things" took central stage, especially in the art and architecture. Stories about ancient Greek automata also provided an inspiration. Marco Polo added his wealth of stories to our new collection. With all these collected stories, the Bible was not the only source of our stories any more. The clergy lost its monopoly over our stories. And we started to weave new stories of our own – ones that were not entirely along lines of the clergy's interpretations of the Bible.

---

80 Although we retrieved our lost stories from Arabs – these were second hand ancient Rome stories we only reintegrated into our cultures and Western civilisation. But in these stories we did not find stories of renewals. And without stories of renewals our cultures and our civilisation are quite young and yet to weave such stories.

81 What have been complex math using roman numerals suddenly became simple and math flourished.

Discoveries of new continents, the printing press, gunpowder, the telescope, the microscope, etc. gave new boosts to the science and philosophy that were no longer dominated by the clergy. Stories that dislodged the Earth as the centre of the universe gained momentum and all this culminated in the 17th Century with stories of Galileo Galilei, Johannes Kepler, Isaac Newton and René Descartes. The universe and all within it seemed to be a much simpler story than Ptolemy's was.

The 17th Century firmly established our, now prevailing, story of a cause and effect driven universe. Everything was believed to be an effect of a prior cause that was, in itself, an effect of a prior cause. And so on, and so on, deeper and deeper into history to the beginning of time and the first cause of everything; the first cause that was not an effect of a prior cause – God[82]. There must be a beginning at the beginning, mustn't there?

---

82 The Big Bang theory is not much more than an attempt to remove God from the same picture of the cause and effect driven universe.

RAPID DEVELOPMENTS OF AUTOMATA CLOSELY followed the rapid pace of philosophy and science. These developments culminated with Jacques de Vaucanson's The Duck – an artificial duck made of gilded copper, which drank, ate, quacked, splashed about in the water and digested its food like a living duck. More importantly, Jacques de Vaucanson invented punched cards to control weaving of cloth. Babbage's analytical engine and Hollerith's census machine (the foundation of IBM) simply followed while René Descartes' considerations of the inner workings of the human being established a powerful theoretical background. As in his considerations (perception → thought → action), all of our contemporary computers are based on a similar principle (input → processing → output).

THE FIRST CRACKS IN THE cause and effect driven universe appeared with Charles Darwin's story. For the first time we had a scientific story without causality in the background. Unfortunately, the grossly misinterpreted theory has landed us in the extreme individualism of our cultures.

George Henry Lewes (an English philosopher of science) further cracked the high glass ceiling set by our old story of a cause and effect driven universe. Although still meeting a stiff opposition, his idea of emerging, rather than derived, properties is earning growing support.

Jules-Henri Poincaré further eroded the story of a cause and effect driven universe. He made significant contributions to the theory of orbits — celestial mechanics — particularly the three-body problem. It turned out that it is impossible to combine solutions of three two-body systems into a single solution for a three-body system, thus turning Kepler's "laws" into approximations. Foundations for entirely different kinds of stories were laid.

Determinists (reductionists as they are called now) fought back bravely, but they had to modify their stories to better fit their observations. The change was cosmetic though: a small devil that spoils an otherwise perfectly predictable outcome. And they called this little devil – chance. And since then we have this excuse for all anomalies in our observations. The excuse we have to believe in, or else… Observing anomalies was close to becoming totally unscientific. And it did in some cases.

THE RECENT TWENTIETH CENTURY BROUGHT 17th Century thought and The Duck
to their extremes. Unfortunately, with benefits came horrible wrongs. Fuelled by the
belief in absolute truth, extremisms of all kinds flourished. And The Duck was em-
bodied in behaviourism that threatened even our own subjectivity – everything was
looked at as a kind of mechanism. At the same time, our extreme individualism dis-
credited and almost completely destroyed our old ethics. Even artists closed their eyes
to peek into our world of sketchy images.

Fortunately, this century further eroded the cause and effect driven universe and
absolute truth stories. Early in the century Kurt Gödel proved that there could be
truths that cannot be proved within a given closed system — truths that cannot be
derived from other truths within a closed system… Carl Gustav Jung joined Gödel
in his way. He established a new story about synchronicity. We had no choice but to
open our eyes and face this infinite universe of ours. Observing anomalies was no
longer a taboo to scientists. And subjectivity was no longer a taboo to Dr. Benjamin
Libet.

The observation of anomalies fully flourished only in the last quarter of the century. This left us with hard to imagine volumes of contradictory data. It is natural that
contradictions emerge from observations of anomalies. But the process of eliminating
shovels and chickens from our stories did not happen.

The dam started to threaten…

Complex Adaptive Systems Theory, Complexity for short, offered a method for
reconciling these contradictions. But very few enthusiastically rolled up their sleeves…
And art was still sleeping and dreaming about superior computers and robots menac-
ing us in all imaginable ways.

Our knowledge cannot self-organise itself on its own. On its own it cannot make order out of the chaos we've made. Our knowledge needs our intents and our vetoes. Our 17th Century stories are tired and they need new life from observed anomalies.

We were stubborn in maintaining our old stories at any cost. And we were negligent towards avalanches of anomalies in our observations. Volumes of documented anomalies are scary and we have no choice now but to roll up our sleeves and clean up the chicken shed.

The best strategy to tackle these scary volumes is to identify the core assumptions that are obviously wrong. Successful challenges will trigger chains of adjustments of our old stories. Most of the accumulated debris will be washed out relatively quickly. The debris left might point at potential core assumptions that might be wrong as well. Tracing them down might be tricky, but it must be done. And we have to work on all this while on the watch for new challenges. Some are already pressing hard, very hard.

Up to now, all my stories were aimed at preparing this battleground. The following stories are challenges to our old stories that are not directly within the Know Thyself Discipline. I have also added some stories as my answers to challenges we are faced with.

The battleground is ready.

OUR ANCIENT CIVILISATION FELL. THE answer to why they fell is now clear. What kept our ancient civilisations together were old answers on old questions. And rigid cultural stories were very fragile. Only cultures that reinvented themselves could keep our civilisation alive.

These renewals could be seen in the evolution of all contemporary civilisations with ancient roots. But our Western civilisation is not one of them – it is barely one thousand years old. We do not have experiences of abandoning our old stories on a massive scale. But do we really need to?

This question is the first symptom of a civilisation which is about to fall – the denial that a novel situation exists (global warming, for example). The second symptom is in offers of old answers to new questions – like the "clean coal" illusion – bury carbon dioxide[83] as rubbish. But the most symptomatic is this perspective – new questions are seen as old questions. And the repetition of old answers for new questions leads our civilisation to its final resting place…

Old answers are not necessarily a bad thing if they require some tweaks and innovation to adjust them to the novel situation. They can become new, but partial answers – like the electric car answer. And these partial answers could buy us time to find and implement complete solutions for novel situations. But to find such solutions we need to cognise the novelty of situations…

And to cognise we need new tools such as the Know Thyself Discipline. We also need a workable ethics and aesthetics. We also need a new dimension for our consciousness – something Europeans started to evolve. But, above all, we need to start weaving new stories that can replace old ones. And all of our stories need to artfully tell more with less – in all aspects of life.

---

83   Three tonnes of carbon dioxide have less than one tonne of carbon we burned and more than two tonnes of oxygen we need to breathe.

THIS MORNING IN A SHOPPING centre, I saw a spoiled brat hysterically crying. Passersby were turning away annoyed. And although mother and child were complete strangers to me, I stepped in. I simply asked the child if she wanted to go with me, rather than with her mother.

In an instant, hysterical cries were replaced with wide-eyed silence and the mother laughed. My intervention was so simple and so effective. And I doubt that the child will resort to hysterical cries in the near future. I think that I did the right thing, didn't I?

I acted according to the first principle of my ethics. I felt personally responsible that there are spoiled brats in my environment. In other words I rejected the "it's not my business" attitude. And I acted to reduce occurrences of hysterical cries in my environment.

Imagine now a world in which everybody would feel personally responsible for hysterical cries of spoiled brats and acted like me. There would not be spoiled brats in our environment. Acting together on the first principle is the second principle of my ethics. And there are only three. This is very simple, workable ethics[84].

My ethics describes good that should emerge from our thoughts, actions or inactions. It outlines criteria for judgement of what is right and what is wrong. It is inevitably idealistic, but it is also a driving force towards what should be.

My ethics demand from me to artfully tell more with less. Artfully, to give emotional charge to my stories to make others to listen. More with less, to make them simple for all to understand. Only the judgements of all of us together can help us to bring about what we all consider to be right and reject what all of us consider being wrong.

*   *   *

There is no room for ideologies, religions, sexisms and other divisions of ours in my ethics. True togetherness demands ultimate respect for all. Our disagreements should not pit us against each other. Our disagreements should challenge us to work together to resolve them.

Shouldn't we all together reject the "it's not my business" attitude? Shouldn't we all together embrace a respectful "it's my business too" attitude of others?

I think that my ethics can help to make our world a better place to live in, don't you?

---

84 Only simple to understand and to follow ethics can offer a fertile ground for intents and vetoes of our consciousness. Without such ethics intents and vetoes of our consciousness will weaken with each controversy faced – and our civilisation will lose ground it is standing on.

BEAUTY IN SCIENCE IS RARELY considered important. But the Know Thyself Discipline does reveal its huge importance. I have already indicated what is beautiful in my previous stories, especially on creativity and on information. But let me start with an example.

If you are used to drawing a line in the dirt for every cow you have, you will think nothing of it. However, to an old Roman your "IIIIIIIIIIIIIIIIII" will look clumsy. He would be much happier with XVIII. And we would be much happier with 2198 rather than with the old Roman's MMCXCVIII. Shorter (simpler) stories are always more beautiful than long ones.

However, simplicity is only one component of beauty. Another one is coherency or harmony between all our stories. If I were a poet, I would use rhyme, rhythm and other tricks of the trade to invoke memories of other stories into every story being told.

The third component of my aesthetics is emotion. Only highly emotionally charged fresh memories can, with the help of empathy, spread beautiful stories through our culture. And this is entirely the opposite of what the scientists' culture demands.

I just read a review of "Sizzle", a comedy released in the USA.[85] The comedy exposed the culture of scientists formed in the Age of Reason and the review predicts, correctly, that scientists will sulk. In the Age of Reason, scientists favoured data and logic and tried to minimise the impact of emotions and imagination. Whole generations were trained to do so, especially in science.

*   *   *

Scientists say that our emotions and daydreaming should not be on the way of our reasoning. And then in the same breath they say that we would not be able to remember, think (reasoning) or act without our emotions.[86] The work of scientists might be tedious but the resulting story should not. We need imagination (creativity) and our emotions in both, work and the resulting story.

These thoughts bring me back to a question I have posed publicly to a number of audiences. Would you consider William Shakespeare to be one of the greatest scientists of all times?

---

85 New Scientist – 23rd of August 2008
86 Another story with shovels and chickens. How to think without having memories?

I certainly do. He doesn't only dwarf all contemporary psychologists, sociologists and anthropologists with his insights into human nature. He also dwarfs them with his ability to communicate his insights to the general public. A truth will always have emotions behind it and only through high emotional charges will it be unveiled to others.

We do need to be artful in making and telling our stories, scientific or otherwise.

As we saw, our civilisations gave rise to social aspect of our consciousness – a perspective to view ourselves as others would see us. This perspective enabled us to be civil to each other and to respect each other. Our consciousness became an integral part of our culture. And it is just like our culture being conscious.

But, do we have a similar intent/veto mechanism for our civilisation? A mechanism that will make our civilisations civil to each other? A mechanism that will make our civilisations respect each other? A consciousness like the consciousness our cultures have?

Unfortunately, in our planetary village, fearful cultures dominate. Our cultures and our civilisations still seek to dominate rather than cooperate. The United Nations was envisioned to work with such consciousness like intent/veto mechanisms, but we do not have such intent/veto mechanisms for our countries and civilisations. We only have webs of intents with habitual thoughts and actions (urges) to pass unchecked.

However, the European Union does seem to be fostering this new dimension in the consciousness of Europeans. Nations do see each other better and cooperate better. And this is filtering down to the consciousness of each individual. The European Union offers a model for the rest of world to follow. If only there were not so many countries eager to dominate and fearful of being dominated... If only there were not ideologies or religions eager to dominate and fearful of being dominated...

Our only hope is in diplomacy. Only patient diplomacy can overcome fears. Only patient diplomacy can quiet these thirsts for domination and fears of being dominated. And I do hope that our rulers will have enough courage to relinquish enough of their powers to diplomats for diplomacy to work.

In the 4th or 5th Century BC, a Chinese general[88] wrote something like this:

> Winners win first[89] and then go to battle.
> Losers go to battle first and then seek a win.

His teachings are taught in military academies all over the world. His teachings are also taught in non-military circles. The Japanese became masters in business negotiations based upon his thought…

But his thought has not been contemplated by our military and political leaders in 2003. The American, British and Australian political and military leaders went into battle first and then scratched their heads…

Our wars are always the result of mistakes we must pay dearly for. And these mistakes are always made long, long before any war of ours erupts. Genocides in Rwanda or in Darfur could have been prevented. Even suicidal extremism could have been prevented…

> Some of our very old stories are too valuable
> and we need to renew them all of the time…

The general managed to tell his story in two short sentences only. I wish I could have such power…

---

87 We also need to be careful what we call war. The war on terror is a typical example. It calls for military effort practically in any part of the world. And this is causing resentment in the stricken parts. The only result we can have here is increased support for criminals and fanatics.

88 Sunzi or Sun-tzu – personal name – Sun Wu.

89 Diplomacy, intelligence, preparations and what to do after the battle – if it comes to the battle at all.

THERE WAS SOMETHING FISHY IN the picture of the cause and effect driven universe. That we could not replicate anything 100% was a worry. The introduction of a little devil that spoils an otherwise perfectly predictable outcome did not make sense at all. Are there hidden causes?

I did not take the issue of causality as a challenge until faced with wild claims about backward in time causality.[90] Mildly said, such claims are irresponsible. Causality in general was in need of close, very close scrutiny…

If every phenomenon in our universe is unique, another phenomenon – supposedly its effect – must also be unique. Causal sequencing of unique phenomena in our open eyes universe could not make any sense.

Causality could only make some sense with repeatable stories (sketches) of our closed eyes universe. Only in our closed eyes universe a story (sketch) about phenomena can be repeated or replicated and a new story about a cause and effect driven universe can be woven. However, did we leave out something important, an anomaly, when we weaved this story of ours?

When I considered Jung's story about synchronicity, four categories of similar phenomena occurring in space and time emerged in my mind:

*   *   *

---

90 Roger Penrose, for example, proposed nanotubes or microtubules to pass information from our consciousness half a second back in time to compensate for Libet's experimentally proven delay. (See his book "The Large, The Small and The Human Mind". Co-authors were Abner Shimony, Nancy Cartwright and Stephen Hawking.) You can test their conjecture with a simple, homemade experiment. Take a long stick and ask a friend to hold it vertically and drop it. You can try to catch it first as fast as possible. In average, you'll catch it in 0.2 seconds. Now try to slow your reactions down. If backward in time suggestion is valid, you should be able to achieve 0.3, 0.4 or 0.5 second reactions. And yet, you will experience reaction times suddenly all above 0.5 seconds. If you were able to catch the stick near the bottom, suddenly you'll be catching it near the top. This experiment has been conducted and replicated with consistent results **before** Dr. Libet finalised his research on timing of our consciousness.

- Similar phenomena emerging with little separation in space and notable separation in time – causality.
- Similar phenomena emerging with notable separation in space and little separation in time – synchronicity.
- Similar phenomena emerging with notable separation in space and time.
- Similar phenomena emerging with little separation in space and time – continuity (identity).

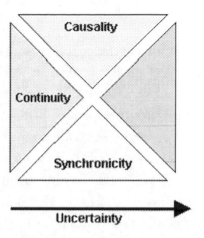

I was ready to put these four categories together in compliance with Complexity Theory. Subsystems of a complex adaptive system do tune themselves to others until a property of the system emerges and stabilises the interplay of its subsystems.

IN OUR OPEN EYES UNIVERSE everything is uncertain – but not because of that little devil called chance. The answer is much simpler: every new phenomenon in our open eyes universe is unique. And if we open our eyes, every new phenomenon will surprise us with its uniqueness, originality, beauty and mystery that often make our closed eyes universe look ridiculous. Unless, of course, we lived too long in our closed eyes universe – surrounded by our old stories and giving old answers on old questions.

We will never be able to entirely predict a unique phenomenon – this is the only certainty we can have. This is the only luxury our open eyes universe can give us. And we need to be grateful for this luxury – for this luxury makes our lives worth living. But can we be less uncertain in the game in which rules are changing all the time?

Yes, we can – by opening our eyes and closely watching how rules change. And rules change depending on how new, emergent phenomena and old already emerged phenomena tune to each other. The tuning that results in resonance between them is what makes each of them unique.

If we open our eyes and start recording how rules change we will have a better idea how they might change in the near future. And we already have a few glimpses at how changes in rules can impact what emerges from them. This is the only way we can lessen our uncertainties. For they are what they are – our uncertainties. And our uncertainties are ours only – they are not uncertainties our open eyes universe might have.

OUR REFLECTIONS ON THE UNIQUE phenomena of our open eyes universe are quite sketchy. Very few lines necessary to outline a phenomenon sufficiently… This sketchiness enables a perceptual approximation – and an apple becomes just another apple. Unique phenomena lose their uniqueness. A vaguer sketch (less lines in the sketch), of fruit for example, will erase differences between apples and grapes.

Out there, in our open, wide open eyes universe, none of our sketches can capture the infinity of details of a unique phenomenon. Out there our sketches and our numbers simply do not make any sense. But in here, they make a world of difference. The only problem in here lies in the always present uncertainty: Did we leave out something important when we were forming our sketches? Did we leave out an anomaly[91]?

Our sketches (stories) outline unique phenomena we experienced before and expect (intent) to experience now. They are old fresh memories turned into our stories – long time memories of ours and of our culture. And every time a phenomenon we map with a story of ours (approximation) – we can remember and count. The closer in time and space the phenomena mapped to the same sketch are, the easier counting will be. And the counting is the first step towards math[92]…

The ability to count otherwise unique phenomena has many advantages. But none of them offers "total" predictability of sensations that will embrace us in the next moment of our lives. Illusionary "total" predictability (safety) can only exist in the cause and effect driven universe of our closed eyes universe…

---

91 Our data will always be shaky no matter how precise our measurements are.
92 Our math unfortunately forgot that 2 are not always 2 – a pair of rabbits can be many rabbits in six months. Also unfortunately, our math forgot the differences between two fruit pieces and two apple pieces – and 1 in 1 = 1 may have different ones…

IN THE 1980S, A LITTLE know scientist Joe Farman, embarrassed NASA scientists. In 1984, the US National Research Council reported that "the ozone layer isn't vanishing after all" This was the same year Joe Farman recorded the biggest hole in the ozone layer over the Antarctic. When his paper was finally published in Nature next year, all hell broke loose.

Soul searching (and embarrassed) scientists first claimed that they did record that sharp drop in ozone concentrations. And that was precisely what they did. But they forgot to tell this to anyone, even to themselves. They simply glossed the records over – as unreliable data or anomalies.[93]

Scientists are intrigued by anomalies, though. But they rarely speak about them openly unless they have a plausible explanation (hypothesis). They would also speak publicly about other anomalies, but only if they consider them relatively irrelevant – like about spacecrafts accelerated by gravitational pull slightly more or less than predicted...

Other, deeply troubling, anomalies seem to not even be thought about...

---

93 Actually, NASA software flagged the data as unreliable – to be fair to the scientists. However, since the scientists specify what software should do, how much software that glosses anomalies over is still running around? Wouldn't we rather have software that will highlight anomalies that can blow our theories apart?

Tomorrow is my birthday, but I already got a present – an agreement between politicians in the US to rescue Wall Street and Main Street. I was lucky that I withdrew my super from investment funds last year. Today, I would be at least 20% shorter and, hopefully, I can release it soon for investment without that loss.

What happened forced me to re-evaluate our old economic stories. As we are wasteful with fossil fuels we are wasteful in just about everything else. And we call this wastefulness our "standard of living." And we want to even increase our living standards (wastefulness). And other countries are racing to catch up with us in wastefulness. There is something inherently wrong in this story of ours…

To find out what is wrong with our economy we need to start with our own behaviour. The careful, introspective, re-evaluation of our behaviour will bring out staggering numbers of shovels and chickens.

We are building as cheaply as possible to make profit as soon as possible. We buy new cars every year – for the industry promotes the car as a status symbol. We buy new cars that guzzle petrol – for the industry promotes the macho image. Only now, the car industry is starting to build fuel efficient cars. And we are still waiting for someone who will start to build long lasting cars that will be cheaper to maintain…

And we love to go to Europe, China and India where cities evolved through millennia – with each generation adding to old and building new in harmony with old. And we love our old cars…

*   *   *

We are now hard pressed by novel situations to re-examine our old stories that are truly inadequate as answers to novel situations. And we have many such wasteful stories in every walk of life. And we need to tackle these wasteful stories with all means imaginable. I will tackle the main ones in the following few little stories.

---

94 In the previous two days I learned about another way of habit breaking exercises – pain. A muscle in my thumb inflamed and most of the habitual moves of my thumb got painful vetos. I was restricted to reading rather than writing. The inflammation is gone today but the memory was still fresh and my thumb needs gentle guidance to restore old habitual moves. However, I do not recommend pain for our habit breaking exercises.

As I'm writing this story, something extraordinary is happening on America's political scene. Even ethics similar to mine have been proposed. This has prompted me to put together my observations about politics.

For a long time we had two opposing political stories: regulate vs. deregulate. They are repeated in power again and again, but in cycles. Whenever one of them starts to hurt, another one is elected into the office – to amend hurts of the previous one.

Our politicians fail here on more than one account. The halls of power blind our politicians to the open eyes universe. They become "out of touch". Ideology, one of these two old stories, also blinds them.

Both of the old stories (ideologies) failed to see that our market is built around good regulations throughout history. Without good regulations we would not enjoy the financial prosperity we enjoy now. Some voters know this and shift the balance of power whenever over-deregulations or over-regulations start to hurt. These voters sense novel situations that require novel answers. And the numbers of those who are tired of both old stories are growing. They either refuse to vote or they watch carefully, very carefully.

Still, most of us vote habitually for one of these two old stories (habits). But the Know Thyself Discipline can help by increasing the numbers of those that are shifting the balance. And, who knows, we might even have a politician who will weave a new story and spell the end to both of the old stories.

*   *   *

We should be aware of the old stories we offer to our politicians. They are often supported by money alone. "Clean coal" is such a story. It is not only expensive and extremely hard to implement on large industrial scales, it can potentially rob us of the oxygen we breathe!

Only a workable ethics can prepare scientists for the Third Millennium. And better science will advise our politicians better. And our politicians will be better prepared for the Third Millennium…

If our legislators start to artfully tell more with less, everybody will better understand their legislations. The need for confused "interpreters" will drop and our administrations and civil services will shed accumulated fat.

US LAWMAKERS FINALLY ADOPTED A rescue plan for Wall Street – adding a bit more certainty to our financial worries.[95] But I have another worry – the story grew to over 450 pages!

We just "packed in" shovels and chickens… for the sake of bipartisanship. There could be more clarity in this when you read these words. But this clarity would be more like a rat out of maze story…

US citizens might not be aware how closely the world is watching their presidential race. I can add my testimony only, but…

What is the rest of the world hoping for? – Leadership.

Leaders do not tell (command) others what to do. Telling others what to do is for managers – not for leaders. Leaders vividly portray their visions for a better future – a future in which everybody can see his place.[96]

The US has managed the rest of the world for far too long – and lost its leadership image. But there is no other leader emerging in the EU or China, for example. And very few want to follow Putin's vision…

I hope that this story will explain to American voters what the rest of the world was hoping for. And I hope that the future US president will read these stories carefully – and act accordingly…

---

95 4th October 2008.
96 Obama's 5th November. You Yankees always lag behind us Australians. You believed it was the 4th whereas it was actually the 5th – in the afternoon, to be precise — when results started to trickle in.

I THINK THAT THE RALLYING call "free market" is nonsense. If we abolished all regulatory restrictions, all of the law actually, all of us would be mugged the next day by greedy muggers waiting around every corner. Those that wish to regulate everything are equally bad – it's simply not possible. Administration would at least triple while we blink...

People always have new ideas. We call this creativity, innovation etc. etc. The same is with the financial markets of our inflated economy. All of our economy is based upon selling as much as possible as fast as possible. And we are even betting on the value of a harvest next year – we call this economic drive...

However, when we are innovative we often see areas of activity others did not notice before. Activity flourishes but very few explore the ethical dimension of the new activity. And here comes the government...

If the ruling ideology is DEREGULATE, nobody will lift a finger. The "free market" will resolve all of its issues. And unchecked, the activity that can be harmful will continue to flourish. We will have a bubbling, vibrant but unchecked economy and bubbles eventually burst.

If the ruling ideology is REGULATE, everybody will jump in to set up a regulation. And even beneficial activities will be stifled, and our economy will wane.

The Market is – the market. It does not care about ideology. It emerged from long histories of good and bad regulations. And even before this time, our parliaments, kings and pharaohs were ruling by decrees to build the foundations for our market. Whenever ethics were not clear it was imposed on our market as legislation.

Shouldn't we build self regulatory ethics into our markets for the Third Millennium? Telling artfully more with less, so that everybody **can** understand would oil such a mechanism even without legislation...

Propping up our governments and markets is only the first step in the right direction. We need more steps in the Third Millennium – we need to prop ourselves up. And the best method that will make us truly serious about our wastefulness should hit our hip pockets – tax.

We should tax every waste – not only pollution.[97] Every car that lasts longer should be taxed less. Every owner should be taxed less for keeping the same car longer. The same waste tax can be implemented for all products and services, including fresh water waste – and savings will prevail over credits. And bombs in our markets will stop ticking…

To enable a transition period and some certainty to ourselves the waste tax can be initially set to zero! A timetable to increase fractions of a percent over twenty or so years would have to be implemented. And the plans should be reviewed every two to three years to adjust the speed of our adjustments…

The waste tax does not need international treaties.[98] All we need is to waste credit exports of goods and services to countries that do not tax waste in a similar way. All we need is to tax waste imports of goods and services from countries that do not tax waste in a similar way. And our countries will be on a steady course to eliminate all waste from our psyche and behaviour.[99]

And where should revenue go? Every waste reducing activity of ours should be rewarded by waste credits. Every innovation that reduces waste should be rewarded by waste credits. And we should be able to sell and buy waste credits. And the new waste credits market will emerge. Our lives will be directed towards sustainable living…

This is how our tax systems can guide us into the Third Millennium…

---

97 In principle, a simple waste tax could eliminate a lot of shovels and chickens from our current tax systems.
98 Some trade treaties would need some renegotiations, though.
99 Poor individuals and nations could be excluded to a degree.

THE ONLY REAL AND FEASIBLE solution for global warming is in photosynthesis. It will capture atmospheric carbon dioxide and release our precious oxygen. And the long-term solution can only be in growing new forests. But we need arable land and fresh water to grow new forests and sources are dwindling, don't we?

The answer lies in humble saltwater algae – and we have plenty of barren land and seawater. We also have plenty of washed away fertilisers to grow them – washed away fertilisers that are creating dead zones in our oceans and are increasing the salinity of our fertile land. And we also have plenty of human waste to grow algae for fertilisers – human waste we took out of the normal biological cycle…

Saltwater algae also desalinate seawater they are growing in. Fleshy ones contain large percentages of fresh water and are good as fertiliser, stock feed[100] or food. With algae we can also grow fish. And, as sweetener, they have very good potential to be a viable source of biofuels.

Apart from rapid capture of atmospheric carbon dioxide, growing seawater algae offers a few more advantages. Growing algae can be done in basins or pods above semi barren land. Basins will shield the soil from the sun, reducing evaporation of fresh water from the soil. Seawater will also evaporate as freshwater vapour further offsetting humidity loss. And algae themselves will provide fresh water and fertilisers to the soil.

Seawater algae cultivation over barren land offers half of the answer for global warming. And my Greening Method (patent pending) offers another half…

* * *

Infertile land can be turned into fertile by growing algae in basins above the ground and in strategically placed ponds. This way, new forests can be grown with farmlands in the mix. Forests will further shield the soil from humidity loss and this might be enough to sustain them without ponds.[101] New forests will also induce vertical air circulation thereby attracting rain where we need it the most. And a lot of new forests inducing vertical air circulation will reduce the chances of violent weather…

---

100 Recently I heard of sheep developing a taste for kelp in absence of fresh grass. I suggested to drought stricken farmers to harvest kelp from the ocean and think about cultivating algae.

101 William Ruddiman suggests that Stone Age farmers halted an ice age in the making. This might be hard to believe, but the evidence now supports his suggestion. All we need now is to do the opposite – and keep a healthy balance.

Such afforestation can gradually cover whole continents with forests. And the long lost rainforest of central Australia could be back again one day.[102] Salinity issues could also be addressed…

Did somebody mention global warming?

---

102 A recent geological dig found evidence of a huge rainforest in central Australia.

WHEN MY OLD COMPANY WAS taken over by CSC, I was given a pile of books as a new method according to which we were to conduct our business! And I fell into disfavour for questioning this "wisdom"…

> The surest way to get people lost is
> to give them piles of shovel-chicken stories!

I'm often stunned by the fuss given to quality control. The story is simplicity in itself: you say what you will do, do it and then map the results with what you said. Simple, isn't it? Hmm…

It entirely depends on what you said you'd do and how you said that you would do it.[103] Precision is fine, but if precision leads you into a mess of shovel-chicken type stories, you'll have a very hard time explaining to your client that it is the chicken not the shovel.

Another danger of precision is in jargon your client does not understand. You might be safe by explaining your jargon to the client later. After all, your client accepted your story told in jargon. But will your client be happy?

And our quality story comes to mine artful telling more with less… The shorter your specification is, the easier each of its elements will be reconcilable with all others. The more artfully you tell your story, the longer fresh memories your client will have. All you need is to carefully add precision without using jargon your client does not understand.[104]

Telling artfully more with less cuts the crap. Could we see some scientists trying to do that? Hmm…

---

103 Technically called specification.
104 Explain your precision in footnotes or appendixes.

There will always be shovels and chickens in our stories.

And we would be wise to let others point at them.

WISE PEOPLE LISTEN, LISTEN VERY carefully and then they sum up what they heard, often in very few sentences that strike a chord in all of us – in all of us who think that we know something. We call these listeners of ours "wise" and they are. They lead by listening.

Unfortunately we are in very short supply of wise people. We have plenty of people who "know" everything – people who ruin states, economies, businesses – and they trust themselves (and we trust them). And we put such people in governance and then it is too late.

The wise people we should trust are those that listen to us. They will change their stories as a sign that they listened to us. And they will tell more with less in their stories. And everybody will understand their stories.

But wise people will never repeat our mantras as their mantras. They will never repeat collective mantras of this or that ideology. They will never repeat collective mantras of this or that god, and they will not tell us what to do. We will know what we need to do as soon they sum us up, and they will lead us by listening to us.

Understanding was never done by thinking.

Understanding was always done by feeling.

THIS MORNING TWO YOUNG PEOPLE of an unknown Christian denomination pestered me. I tried to be polite, knowing what was about to happen. As expected, the first question was do I believe in God. Although I knew what would follow I had no choice but to say no. If I said yes, the conversation would inevitably lead towards: **which one**? I managed to politely say good-bye with a sour taste in my mouth.

Let's face it. We are either atheists or polytheists. Atheists believe that there is no god.[105] The rest of us are either honest or dishonest polytheists. And dishonest polytheists proclaimed themselves to be believers in the one and only god.

And we became true believers. We left no room for another, one and only, god. And, in the name of our "one and only" god, we even killed and maimed. And, in the name of our "one and only" god, we are creating prolife movements while taking life to stuff ourselves into obesity – for our "one and only" god gave us our universe to use and abuse.

I cannot and I will not honour any of these "one and only" gods
with a capital G.

Although Christianity gave up sword and witch-hunt to spread, it invented missionaries. Missionaries are deeply religious and honest in their activities. But they are, knowingly or not, like party activists. Do we have divine elections? I mean, do we have to choose which god of our gods is the one – the only one?

I have no choice but to say no to any of these gods. Neither of these gods is my God. Only occasionally can I reach a degree of agreement with a religious person about God. All the rest is empty talk full of old stories endlessly repeated for thousands of years.

* * *

I do not like to call my God – God, for I know what the waiting question will be: Which one? This is why I prefer to call my God – universe; one and only. The infinite universe full of unique phenomena... The universe full of mysteries... The universe evolving in each moment... And each moment emerging from the previous, builds up upon the previous giving us an impression of time. And this universe embraces me with an infinite richness of sensations every moment of my life.

I better stop here. Otherwise I'm in danger of sounding like those two young missionaries. My God can be only lived in. My God cannot be talked or preached about.

---

105 It's rather a sceptics' "inconclusive" rebuke.

My God must not be in danger of becoming an old story, for every moment of my life my God is a New God – forever. My greatest story will never be fully told…

I'll be happy if your God is like mine. Wouldn't we all be happier with many gods like mine? Believers will be much happier living in such a universe. Non-believers will be much happier believing in such a universe. And we all will be much happier with such a polytheistic universe – at least until we all agree that it is the same God.

And the God we broke into pieces will be one and whole again.

First of all – thank you very much for reaching this page.

EXCEPT COMPLEXITY THEORY RELATED STORIES, I have told all of my stories I intended to for this project.[106] But I also have another project – You. And this project of mine cannot be successful without You – I need to make it plain now.

You may have patiently went through this book finding some stories that might have had — just might have had — a few valid points… If You did find some, they will now be with You, providing momentary pauses to re-evaluate them. And these re-evaluations will bring You back to this book.

Repeated reading will give You another few valid points – points You did not notice before. Thoughts that might have been difficult to think about will appear more natural now and some old thoughts of Yours might appear a bit strange — worthy of closer scrutiny. And You will start to write Your own stories telling artfully more with less. And both of US will face this third millennium together…

My Stories should not be repeated endlessly. They are not intended to last forever… They are written to make You think. As soon you weave better ones – Your Stories should replace mine.

Thank You again,
Damir Ibrišimović

---

106 I had to leave out many other stories because clarity would be lost. Artfully telling more with less might shrink these stories in the future enough to leave room to integrate more stories.

ALL OF MY STORIES HAVE a single theoretical background – Complex Adaptive Systems Theory or Complexity for short. But don't be deterred – complexity is in its name only. What is challenging is its strangeness, though. I will therefore try to simplify this story I altered a bit. If you still feel uncomfortable with it now, come back later. Please.

George Henry Lewes (an English philosopher of science) distinguished between phenomena that are predictable from their constituent parts and phenomena that are not - emergence (such as salt which looks nothing like sodium or chlorine). Jules-Henri Poincaré made significant contributions to the theory of orbits – celestial mechanics — particularly the three-body problem. It turned out that it is impossible to combine solutions of three two-body systems into a single solution for a three-body system, thus turning Kepler's "laws" into approximations.

Although without explanations, those we now call reductionists fought this notion until the 1970s. Reductionists started to lose their theoretical ground. Reductionists did not manage to derive saltiness from properties of sodium or chlorine, not to mention left or right orientations of some carbohydrates.

The old stories (that we will explain everything just by looking at its components) are being replaced by a new story. From the chaotic quantum arena to our world of infinities, at every step, new properties emerge. These are new properties that cannot be derived from properties of their components – like water. This new story tells us that order emerges in complex adaptive systems from disorder. And this new story also offers a mathematical platform to stand on.

The Complexity Theory introduces new concepts and understanding them is essential. The basic concepts are listed and explained in the following story with alternative words and expressions (in brackets) that are used to facilitate other stories.

IT IS IMPORTANT TO NOTE that in the Complexity Theory[107] we do not have sequences of events or cause and effect relations but rather all elements of the system and the system itself tuning to each other until equilibrium (or resonance) is found. The equilibrium is defined as one of one or more energetically lower and stable states of the entire system.

Energy Level   Falls into roughly three categories in which the system has 1) energy levels that keep the system oscillating between few, potentially stable states; 2) threshold energy levels at which the system is about to fall into one of the stable states and; 3) energy levels that are below the threshold.

Emergent Property   (Attribute, resonance or equilibrium) one of (likely) more than one stable states (resonances) in which the system as a whole can be. If sufficient energy is introduced into the system as a whole (to raise energy level above threshold) it will start to oscillate between states again. The stable system exhibits one (emergent property) of few potential properties, i.e. it resonates in one of few potential resonances. (Note emergence of distinctive from continuum.)

Symmetry Splitting   The system can contain various levels of energy, some of which are above a certain threshold and keep the system oscillating between potential stable states. When the energy level of the system drops to the threshold level, the symmetry splitting occurs and the system is stabilised.

---

107 Complexity Theory also puts a big question mark over quantum physics. If we are not able to derive emerged properties from properties of constituent parts, can we derive properties of constituent parts from properties of the system. And the whole quantum physics is based upon inferring properties of constituent parts (wavicles) from the results of their interplays.

Agent

(Oscillator, element of the system or subsystem) Subsystem of the system that impacts other subsystems is called agent. The agent impacts (tunes) other agents within the system while being itself impacted (tuned) by others at the same time.

Tuning

(Impact or interplay) (Re-)action of an agent (oscillator) towards other agents coupled with (re-actions) of other agents (oscillators). The tuning as a process ends with a resonance within the system. It could also be related to falling energy levels of the system until a stable state is reached. I have added this concept to explain the method used by agents to bring about a "collective" outcome. Information does not travel faster than light. Neither do agents react so fast. Each agent needs then to tune its internal clock to others "guessing" when others will make their tick and tack. Only then can agents start to tick in unison.

THE BEHAVIOUR OF THE COMPLEX adaptive system could be imagined as roulette. A small ball spinning can represent energy levels. The roulette disk should be imagined as having one or more dents or valleys between the edge and the centre. These valleys could be of various depths representing energy drops a stable system could have.

Inevitably, the ball starts to jump in and out of valleys, losing energy. Although deeper valleys and valleys closer to the edge have higher chances to trap the ball, the ball still can end up in others. When the ball is finally trapped in one of the valleys, the symmetry is split and the system becomes stable, exhibiting one (of potentially few) emergent properties.[108]

A system could be always seen as a subsystem. There is continuous energy flow in and out (tuning with the environment). If the former prevails, the system is increasingly destabilised until energy levels rise above the threshold. The opposite happens if energy flow out prevails.

Theoretically there is infinity of subsystem/system levels. It would be neither wise nor practical to put any limits. However, a "cut" into a few levels is always possible and at our "level" quite manageable.

These complexity stories are my adjustment of Klaus Mainzer's. The theory he offered lacked tuning.

---

108 Note the transition of continuity into discrete.

Infinity & Seeing

We have only one utterly subjective experiment to verify these stories: opening and closing our own eyes and noticing the difference. Nobody else will be able to notice this difference observing us as we open and close our eyes. However, if we all perform this experiment and honestly admit that there is an enormous difference, we might agree with this observation. And this observation will have to be accepted by scientists – as a scientific observation. Other indirect support is offered by answers to questions like: why can't we replicate anything 100%?

Us

Unlike with Infinity and Seeing, talking about us is much easier. Scientists already confirmed that there is no difference in brain activity between imagined and actually seen images. Additional experiments to confirm or refute this story are welcome, though.

The Scientific Method

I HOPE THAT THIS IS a pretty good summation of the method. Although scientists themselves have already admitted some deficiencies, they are not yet familiar with our sensations being altered. From a physicist to a policeman, we need to weed out the inevitable alterations our professions impose. And this can be done only by those that are not our peers.

Know Thyself

I SINCERELY HOPE THAT PEOPLE will start introspective experimentations; people from all walks of life. The Know Thyself Discipline can improve performance and teaching/learning new skills in all walks of life. The Know Thyself Discipline might be as ancient as our humanity is – and in science it found a new life.

Knowing ourselves better enables us to know others better, firming the foundations of our understanding.

Little Us in Charge

History – and we better leave it there.

Recognition, Cognition, Non-conscious Cognition

Psychologists already have plenty of observations about how we recognise and cognise. However, the notion that we have a learning process in terms of what to expect on unfamiliar ground sheds new light on the current findings and offers new criteria for future observations.

I would suggest experiments in which subjects can be shown short movies of a familiar or unfamiliar place. Measuring the activity of the eyes combined with brain scans could provide a wealth of data to determine differences. Monitoring the behaviour of different sets of subjects in actual situations could provide more data.

Non-conscious cognition cannot be confirmed by experiments. Here we can only collect the observations of psychologists and psychiatrists after an event.

Rhythm, Emotions & Empathy

APART FROM DETERMINING THE IMPORTANCE of emotions for our memory and their impact on our metabolism, scientific research is very poor. However, there is excellent research done practically (and introspectively) by artists, especially by stage actors and their teachers. Unfortunately, very good actors are more interested in acting than in theories about how we transfer our emotions and the rhythm behind this transfer. And those that are not very good actors cannot articulate them per definition.

I had no choice but to closely observe great actors and their impact. My early engagement with professionals also helped me to reach some conclusions and start giving partial answers. But I admit that a much wider discussion is needed here. I invite, therefore, artists and scientists to fill the gaps.

Intent

Intent can trigger only habitual stories, unless it is altered through empathy. This hides a hidden danger reflected in how we recognise, for example. If we are used to recognising a pyramid from above only, we will fail to recognise the transparent pyramid from below. Somebody has to tell us that another perspective (story, symbol) is possible and this will trigger a learning-like process. Only when we get used to the new perspective will the intent to change a perspective result in seeing the intended with the usual half a second delay. This can be tested by measuring the time.

Intent can also be tested with brain scans of subjects when they observe ambiguous images. In the offered example, there should be detectable differences between up and down with probably less detectable differences between obscure and transparent. Other ambiguous images will probably show other differences between sketchy images.

Brain activity of intent itself might be hard to detect. However, if we do enough comparisons between brain activities of involuntary moves with no intents behind and voluntary moves with intents behind, we might detect differences. I suspect that there are only a few cells active for intent.

Free and Not So Free Will

DR. BENJAMIN LIBET ALREADY PROVIDED sufficient evidence for veto related parts of these two stories. However, based on the subjective experiences, I did add an important component to his story – intent. This could be tested by comparing scans before and after the subject is directed to change intent. Direction to move a body part could be changed into utter "apple" when they feel the urge. In another series of experiments we can leave the subject to decide when to change the intent.

Measurements during a walk on familiar and unfamiliar territory could also provide some insights. Amplified differences in brain activity could make visible webs of intents we have on familiar territory.

I would also suggest an intriguing experiment with subjects who strongly believe in causality. Psychologists could gather quite interesting data while subjects read my story on the topic. A condition would be, of course, that they did not read this book yet.

Weaving New Stories

OUR STORIES GIVE A SHAPE to everything we see in our open eyes universe. We must be aware that what we see is actually shaped to fit to our stories. It is therefore important to notice dynamics between both the open and closed eyes universes. This is where the Know Thyself Discipline begins.

Some may say that the case of Jill Price, who suffers from hyperthymestic syndrome[109], might shed some doubt on this story of mine. I would argue the contrary. In her case it seems that her fresh memories lose their emotional charge significantly more slowly. This may have impacted reconciliation with her fresh memories (ways of how we forget). Disharmony between her fresh memories is a probable reason why she writes that her memories haunt her. I admit, however, that more research is needed to settle the issue.

Scientists trained themselves for far too long to eliminate emotions from their work. This has done more damage to science than anything else. More than anything else, emotions are the initial drivers that turn stories of others into our stories and our stories into stories of others. Not telling artfully more with less simply invites others to drop our stories…

Other evidence combined with Libet's findings confirms most of this story. However, my suggestion about fresh memories being emotionally charged potential stories has only indirect evidence. My clear-cut criterion does offer a solid base for further research. Cases of hyperlexia also strongly indicate a possibility that literacy related sketchy images can filter into our genes. All this needs much more research.

---

109 The inability to forget and the ability to remember events almost as they happened a moment ago.

Thinking

THIS STORY CAN BE TESTED partly directly and partly indirectly. Since we can determine from scans that the subject is thinking about a person, I suggest the following. The brains of subjects who are in love should be scanned while performing a mental task. In the middle of the task they should be asked about their loved one. After this they should be instructed to perform the task, but also to let their thoughts to wander at will.

The comparison should provide enough data to determine important differences between a wandering and a focused brain. For other possible tests we might need to wait for new techniques and technologies.

Growing Up

PSYCHOLOGISTS AND TEACHERS HAVE ALREADY provided some supporting data. I would suggest, though, including observations of effects of outside intents (stimulations) and of outside vetoes.

"Shovel-Chicken Stories", Creativity & Humour

THIS STORY CAN BE TESTED with the same subjects over a longer period. At the beginning they should be given new stories with various degrees of emotional charge while their brain is being scanned. (Emotional charge could also be estimated by quizzing the subjects on the topics before. The next morning they should be quizzed about which stories they remember and to assess the vividness of their dreams overnight. They should be given habit breaking exercises to perform until the next cycle begins. Taking walks to relax, not to exercise, should be suggested. The same should be performed in a few sessions at regular intervals of not less than a fortnight.

Expected results are:

1.   More stories with lesser emotional charge remembered.
2.   Better remembered dreams.

The results will probably be rather indicative. But they could provide us with clues to devise better experiments.

This experiment could be complemented by training subjects to remember their dreams better. How this may improve our creativity is not clear yet, but comparisons with only habit breaking technique data could give us insights for further research.

This experiment could also be complemented with exercises to improve our observational skills. Although it is likely that an increase in creativity will enhance observational skills, the improvement will be hard to measure. However, improvements in observational skills compared with improvements assessments without creativity exercises could provide some indications.

Reason, Truth & Absolute Truth

I WILL LEAVE THIS INTENTIONALLY blank…

Disinformation & Information

THE BLUNDER OF THE "INFORMATION" industry about what is information is clear to anybody who tried to tackle the problem seriously. It was funny to watch physicists quickly changing their spin when the speed of light was questioned. Suddenly they spoke about the speed of information as a constant. Now they are silent. Maybe somebody whispered them about Kolmogorov's math…

The information story might be tested by experiments devised for other stories. It might be possible to detect reductions in areas of the brain activity of subjects focused on a topic after the challenges of new stories have been resolved. However, such measurements might be difficult in practice.

The best indications we might obtain by simulations of our closed eyes universe. As chicken and shovels are eliminated during reconciliation of a new story with old ones, we are likely to witness shrinkage of data within our model.

Know Thyself Theory, Scientific Observation

WILLY-NILLY BOTH, SCIENTISTS AND NON-SCIENTISTS, reflect upon their fresh memories – fresh memories scientists classify as data or as other, normal, fresh memories. Scientists might be a bit more methodical in sifting data, but the absence of the knowledge that they are doing it introspectively puts them at the same disadvantage non-scientists have. And Know Thyself Theory can return some balance to both. A healthy Sceptic story could do the rest of the trick…

We should also keep in mind that we all interpret sensations we are enveloped with on the basis of our culture and our previous experiences. Willy-nilly, scientific data are also results of such interpretations and, as such, might deviate from what we actually experienced.

Evolution & Life

EVIDENCE OF "STORY" EXCHANGES HAS been offered across biological disciplines. I have put them all together to propose "inner" evolution as a driver for changes in our genome and physical form. I hope for a lot of discussions re this proposal. (You can make a few notes here.)

Beginnings without Beginnings

TOGETHER WITH THE FOLLOWING STORIES I outlined a possible mental and cultural evolution – transformation we experienced during our early migrations. I hope for your comments here…

The Second Millennium

THIS IS MY VIEW OF the history of our Western culture – your thoughts?

The Third Millennium

WHAT DO YOU SEE COMING?

Ethics & Aesthetics

Other Comments from You, Please

http://users.zipworld.com.au/~damir

I'M NEITHER A SCIENTIST NOR a philosopher. I was, though, a consultant in the computing industry almost all my working life. And in such position I had to practice reconciling, often conflicting[110], old stories from all walks of life on a daily basis. With such experiences I have turned into a very keen listener and observer. And my interest in almost all scientific disciplines leads me to attempts to apply my reconciling skills in the science as well.

Ten years ago I published the first set of my little (scientific) stories on the web. I called the collection "Imagination is Greater than Knowledge". I have maintained my website for five years, but the whole structure needed a revamp, since my thoughts had evolved further. And although relating the stories on the web is much easier, it holds a hidden danger – Internet readers are less inclined to be comprehensive and thoughtful than readers of a printed book.

Book format for my stories imposed new restrictions on the structure of my stories. I also had to shrink them even more to artfully tell more with less. I'm not so sure how artful they are, but I succeeded to tell more with less.

Telling stories about us needs a historical dimension also – how we became what we are now – our perceptual and mental evolution. For, it seems obvious that some 250,000 years ago we neither saw nor thought as we do now. Furthermore, such perspective may give us inklings into trends that might guide our future evolution…

We are already pressed hard to make some mental leaps of faith. How well I outlined them by proposed "know thyself" discipline – you are to judge. You are also the judge of all other related stories of mine, but you do not need to be a lawyer to judge here. You do not even have to be a scientist to judge here. All you need is common sense. I did my best to eliminate any need for the rest.

---

110 Cleaning up chicken sheds…

Damir Ibrišimović

(**Du**st-**mi**racle **E**-**bri**ck-**ship**-**mo**re-**which**)

I HATE TO TALK ABOUT myself as somebody else would. As if somebody else would talk about me more objectively… But, let's cut a long story short.

I was born in Zagreb, on the 30ᵗʰ September 1949 at 10 o'clock in the evening (if you wish to make me a horoscope). The usual primary and high schools were followed by the usual disorientation of the youth of my age. Since army service was mandatory, I was serving when the Croatian Spring of 1971 happened. (Not very pleasant to be Croat then…) My subsequent study of general linguistics and indology was crowned by the opening of a new group of subjects. And I became one of the proud founders of Information Sciences, which I enrolled in immediately.

I was working in the computing industry even before I completed my studies. That would make more than thirty years of experience when I was forced into early retirement.

There are many other aspects of me that can shed much better light on me than just a chronology. But they are hidden in my stories. And I hope that they will please you as you read them…